API DEVELOPMENT FUNDAMENTALS WITH FLASK

Unlocking The Power Of Flask For API Development

KRISTINE ELLIS

TABLE OF CONTENTS

Chapter 1: Introduction to Flask and API Development

1.1 What is Flask and Why Choose It for API Development?

Flask is a popular, lightweight web framework for Python that is known for its simplicity and flexibility. Unlike some other full-fledged frameworks like Django, Flask follows a minimalistic philosophy, providing just the essentials for building web applications. This "microframework" approach allows developers to have complete control over their projects, providing a flexible structure that can be easily extended with third-party libraries and tools.

At its core, Flask provides routing, templates, and simple support for various web technologies. However, it leaves the decision-making regarding how to structure your project, which database to use, and how to handle additional features to the developer. This gives Flask the advantage of being highly customizable and suitable for a wide range of use cases, including API development.

So why choose Flask for API development?

1. Lightweight and Flexible

One of the key reasons developers favor Flask for API development is its lightweight nature. While larger frameworks may come with pre-configured tools and plugins, Flask's minimalism ensures that developers start with only the features they need. This allows for a clean, simple API design without unnecessary overhead. For example, Flask doesn't enforce specific patterns or project structures, enabling you to mold your app the way you see fit. This simplicity makes Flask ideal for small to medium-sized projects, and it can scale up as needed.

2. Easy to Learn and Use

Flask's design philosophy emphasizes simplicity and ease of use. With minimal boilerplate code, beginners can dive into Flask with little learning curve. The framework has clear and concise documentation, and there is a large community of developers actively contributing tutorials, tips, and open-source projects. Flask provides intuitive routing, URL handling, and response structures that make building RESTful APIs a breeze.

3. Full Control and Customizability

Unlike frameworks that enforce specific tools or approaches, Flask offers you full control over how your application works. This flexibility is especially beneficial for API development, where specific functionality may be required. For instance, if you need to integrate a unique database system or a custom authentication method, Flask allows you to choose the best libraries and plug them into your application with minimal friction.

4. Integration with Extensions

Flask's microframework nature doesn't mean you have to build everything from scratch. Flask has a vast ecosystem of extensions that provide additional functionalities. For example:

- **Flask-SQLAlchemy**: A powerful SQL toolkit and Object-Relational Mapper (ORM) for working with databases.
- **Flask-RESTful**: A simple extension for building REST APIs.
- **Flask-JWT-Extended**: A Flask extension for working with JSON Web Tokens (JWT) to implement authentication in your APIs.
- **Flask-CORS**: For handling Cross-Origin Resource Sharing (CORS), which is crucial when developing APIs for the web.

These extensions make it easy to integrate additional features into your project without reinventing the wheel. You can choose the tools that best suit your project's needs.

5. Excellent for RESTful APIs

Flask is a natural fit for developing RESTful APIs. The framework's core functionality allows you to map URLs to Python functions, making it easy to handle HTTP methods (GET, POST, PUT, DELETE, etc.). With the help of extensions like Flask-RESTful, developers can quickly build APIs that are easy to manage, extend, and scale.

6. Scalability and Performance

Despite being lightweight, Flask can scale efficiently. You can start with a small project and later enhance the application as the demand for your API grows. Flask also provides

2

support for asynchronous programming, which can handle multiple requests simultaneously without blocking. Additionally, it integrates well with other systems, databases, and tools, ensuring that as your application expands, Flask will continue to meet performance needs.

7. Strong Community Support

Flask has a vibrant, active community that continues to support and improve the framework. With numerous online forums, tutorial websites, and open-source contributions, you won't have to look far to find help when you need it. From simple code examples to advanced problem-solving, the Flask community is an invaluable resource for API developers.

8. Python Ecosystem Compatibility

Since Flask is built on Python, it takes full advantage of the vast Python ecosystem. You can easily integrate with machine learning libraries like TensorFlow or scikit-learn, data analysis libraries like Pandas, or cloud platforms like AWS and Google Cloud. This allows Flask to not only handle web API tasks but also integrate seamlessly into larger data-driven projects.

9. Robust Testing Capabilities

Flask offers built-in support for unit testing, which is crucial for API development. You can test individual API endpoints, mock requests, and ensure that your application performs as expected before deploying it to production. Testing is a vital step in API development, and Flask's support for testing makes it a preferred framework for developers looking to ensure reliability and stability.

10. Ideal for Prototyping and MVPs

Flask's simplicity and speed make it a go-to framework for rapidly prototyping APIs and creating Minimum Viable Products (MVPs). If you're looking to quickly build and iterate on an API-based application, Flask can get you from concept to working code in record time. Its flexibility allows you to tweak and improve your API as you gather user feedback, making Flask an excellent choice for startups and small teams.

1.2 The Basics of Web Development

Web development is the process of creating and maintaining websites and web applications. It involves everything from building simple static pages to developing complex dynamic systems that interact with users, databases, and external services. At its core, web development can be divided into three key components: **front-end development**, **back-end development**, and **database management**. Understanding the basics of web development is crucial for anyone looking to create web-based applications, including APIs.

1.2.1 Front-End Development

Front-end development is the part of web development that involves everything the user sees and interacts with on a website or web application. This includes the design, layout, and structure of the user interface (UI). Front-end developers work with technologies like HTML, CSS, and JavaScript to create responsive, visually appealing pages.

- **HTML**: The structure of the web page is built using HTML (HyperText Markup Language). HTML defines the different sections of a page, such as headers, paragraphs, images, links, and forms.
- **CSS**: Cascading Style Sheets (CSS) is used to style the HTML content. It controls the colors, fonts, layout, and overall look of the page. Responsive design is often achieved using CSS frameworks like Bootstrap or Flexbox.
- **JavaScript**: JavaScript is a programming language that adds interactivity to a webpage. It allows developers to create dynamic content, handle user interactions, and manage data asynchronously (using AJAX or Fetch API).

Front-end developers must ensure that a web page is not only functional but also user-friendly, intuitive, and visually appealing. They also need to ensure that the page is responsive, meaning it adapts well to different screen sizes, from mobile devices to large desktop monitors.

1.2.2 Back-End Development

Back-end development refers to the server-side of web development. It involves building the logic, databases, and server configurations that power the front-end experience. The back-end is responsible for processing requests, retrieving and storing data, and handling the flow of information between the server and the front-end.

- **Web Servers**: Web servers like Apache, Nginx, or Flask handle incoming HTTP requests from clients (users) and serve responses. These servers are essential for handling the communication between users and the web application.
- **Programming Languages**: Back-end developers use server-side programming languages to build the application logic. Common languages include Python (with Flask or Django), Ruby (with Rails), PHP, JavaScript (with Node.js), and Java (with Spring Boot).
- **APIs**: One of the main roles of the back-end is to expose APIs that allow the front-end to interact with the server. APIs (Application Programming Interfaces) allow different software systems to communicate and exchange data.
- **Authentication and Security**: The back-end is responsible for managing user authentication (e.g., logging in) and securing sensitive data. It ensures that the right people can access certain resources and that user information is protected.

Back-end development also includes managing databases, which are used to store and retrieve data. Databases are essential for dynamic web applications where user-generated content, such as blog posts, comments, or product listings, needs to be stored.

1.2.3 Databases and Data Management

Databases are a critical component of web development, as they allow applications to store, retrieve, and manage data efficiently. There are two primary types of databases:

- **Relational Databases (SQL)**: These databases store data in tables with predefined schemas and relationships between tables. Common SQL databases include MySQL, PostgreSQL, and SQLite. SQL (Structured Query Language) is used to query and manage the data.
- **NoSQL Databases**: NoSQL databases are more flexible and store data in formats like JSON, key-value pairs, or documents. They are useful for applications with rapidly changing or unstructured data. Common NoSQL databases include MongoDB, Redis, and CouchDB.

Back-end developers often work closely with databases to ensure that data is stored efficiently, queried effectively, and protected against issues like data corruption or unauthorized access.

5

1.2.4 Understanding HTTP and APIs

The foundation of web development revolves around the HTTP protocol, which is used for communication between the client (user's browser) and the server. HTTP stands for HyperText Transfer Protocol, and it defines how requests and responses are sent over the web.

When a user enters a URL in their browser, the browser sends an HTTP request to the web server. The server processes this request, retrieves the necessary data, and sends back an HTTP response. This response might contain the HTML of a webpage, an image, or data formatted in JSON or XML.

An **API (Application Programming Interface)** is an intermediary that allows different applications to communicate with each other. In the context of web development, an API exposes certain functions or data of an application so that other programs can access them. APIs are typically built using HTTP and follow certain conventions like REST (Representational State Transfer), which defines how APIs should be structured and how resources (data) should be represented.

Web development involves creating the structure, functionality, and logic for web applications. It combines front-end technologies, back-end technologies, and databases to provide a seamless user experience. For API development, understanding these basics is essential, as APIs form the backbone of modern web applications, enabling communication between different systems and services. With frameworks like Flask, developers can focus on building clean, efficient, and scalable APIs that drive web applications.

1.3 Overview of RESTful APIs

A **RESTful API** (Representational State Transfer) is an architectural style used for designing networked applications. It operates over HTTP and relies on a set of well-defined principles to ensure that the interactions between the client and server are stateless, scalable, and efficient. REST has become the go-to approach for building APIs because of its simplicity and its ability to handle complex, distributed systems.

Core Principles of REST

RESTful APIs adhere to several core principles, each contributing to the ease of use and scalability of these APIs. These principles include:

- **Statelessness**: Every request made by the client to the server must contain all the necessary information for the server to understand and fulfill the request. The server does not store any client context between requests. This means that each request is independent, and no session information is stored between requests.
- **Client-Server Architecture**: In a RESTful system, the client and the server are separate entities. The client handles the user interface and user interaction, while the server manages the application data and business logic. This separation of concerns allows for better scalability and maintainability.
- **Uniform Interface**: RESTful APIs have a consistent and standardized interface. This uniformity simplifies the learning curve for developers and ensures that APIs are easily understood and used. Resources are accessed through URLs, and interactions with resources are performed using standard HTTP methods (GET, POST, PUT, DELETE).
- **Cacheability**: REST APIs allow responses to be explicitly marked as cacheable or non-cacheable, enhancing performance by reducing the need for repetitive requests. If responses can be cached, they can be stored and reused for subsequent requests, saving time and resources.
- **Layered System**: REST APIs can be organized into layers, where each layer has a specific responsibility, such as authentication, caching, or load balancing. This structure allows for greater flexibility and scalability in handling large-scale applications.
- **Code on Demand (Optional)**: Although not commonly used, REST allows the server to transfer executable code (like JavaScript) to the client. This feature can be used for improving client-side functionality without requiring an additional round-trip to the server.

HTTP Methods and RESTful API Operations

A RESTful API operates by using standard HTTP methods to perform operations on resources, which are typically represented by URLs (Uniform Resource Locators). The primary HTTP methods include:

- **GET**: Retrieves data from the server. It is used to fetch resources without modifying them.
- **POST**: Sends data to the server to create a new resource.
- **PUT**: Updates an existing resource on the server with new data.
- **DELETE**: Removes a resource from the server.
- **PATCH**: Partially updates an existing resource.

For example, let's say we have an API for managing a collection of books. The following HTTP methods could be used:

- **GET /books**: Retrieves a list of all books.
- **POST /books**: Adds a new book to the collection.
- **GET /books/{id}**: Retrieves the details of a specific book.
- **PUT /books/{id}**: Updates the details of a specific book.
- **DELETE /books/{id}**: Deletes a specific book from the collection.

Each resource (in this case, books) is represented by a unique URL, and the operations on the resource are performed using the appropriate HTTP methods. This simplicity makes RESTful APIs a favorite for web applications, mobile apps, and IoT devices.

Status Codes and RESTful APIs

HTTP status codes play a crucial role in RESTful APIs by communicating the outcome of a request. These codes indicate whether the request was successful, whether errors occurred, and what type of error occurred. Common HTTP status codes include:

- **200 OK**: The request was successful, and the server returned the requested data.
- **201 Created**: A new resource was successfully created on the server.
- **204 No Content**: The request was successful, but there is no content to return (used in DELETE or PUT requests).
- **400 Bad Request**: The request was malformed or missing required parameters.
- **401 Unauthorized**: The client must authenticate itself to access the resource.
- **403 Forbidden**: The client does not have permission to access the resource.
- **404 Not Found**: The requested resource was not found on the server.
- **500 Internal Server Error**: The server encountered an unexpected error and was unable to process the request.

By following the REST architecture and using appropriate HTTP status codes, developers can create intuitive and user-friendly APIs that are easy to integrate with client-side applications.

1.4 Setting Up Your Flask Environment

Before you begin developing your API using Flask, you need to set up the environment where your Flask application will run. Flask is built on Python, so it's essential to have a working Python environment on your machine. Below are the steps to set up a Flask development environment:

Step 1: Install Python

First, make sure that Python is installed on your machine. Flask requires Python 3.5 or newer. You can check if Python is installed by running the following command in your terminal or command prompt:

bash

CopyEdit

```
python --version
```

If Python is not installed, you can download it from the official Python website.

Step 2: Create a Virtual Environment

It's recommended to use a virtual environment when developing with Flask to isolate your project dependencies from your global Python environment. A virtual environment is a self-contained directory that contains a Python installation and all the packages you need for a project.

To create a virtual environment, navigate to your project directory and run the following commands:

bash

CopyEdit

```
# On Windows

python -m venv venv


# On macOS/Linux

python3 -m venv venv
```

This will create a new folder called venv where your virtual environment will be stored. To activate the virtual environment:

Windows:
bash
CopyEdit

```
venv\Scripts\activate
```

- **macOS/Linux**:
  bash
  CopyEdit

  ```
  source venv/bin/activate
  ```

Once activated, your terminal prompt will change to indicate that you are working within the virtual environment. Any packages you install using pip will be installed in this isolated environment.

Step 3: Install Flask

With your virtual environment active, you can now install Flask. Run the following command:

bash

CopyEdit

```
pip install Flask
```

This will download and install the latest version of Flask from the Python Package Index (PyPI).

Step 4: Create a Basic Flask Application

Now that Flask is installed, let's create a simple Flask application. In your project directory, create a new file named app.py and add the following code:

python

CopyEdit

10

```
from flask import Flask


app = Flask(__name__)


@app.route('/')

def hello_world():

    return 'Hello, World!'

if __name__ == '__main__':

    app.run(debug=True)
```

This code creates a Flask application with a single route (/) that returns the string "Hello, World!" when accessed. To run the application, execute the following command in your terminal:

bash

CopyEdit

```
python app.py
```

Your Flask application will start running locally on port 5000 by default. You can access it in your browser by navigating to http://127.0.0.1:5000.

Step 5: Install Development Tools

For efficient Flask development, consider installing additional tools like:

- **Flask-RESTful**: An extension for building REST APIs with Flask.
- **Flask-Cors**: A Flask extension for handling Cross-Origin Resource Sharing (CORS).
- **Flask-SQLAlchemy**: For database integration with Flask using SQLAlchemy.

You can install these tools using pip:

bash

CopyEdit

```
pip install Flask-RESTful Flask-Cors Flask-SQLAlchemy
```

This will allow you to extend the basic Flask functionality to support more advanced API features like authentication, database interactions, and CORS management.

1.5 Flask Project Structure and Best Practices

Flask is a flexible framework, allowing developers to structure their applications in a variety of ways. However, adhering to a consistent and scalable project structure can help ensure your app remains maintainable as it grows. Here's a breakdown of how to organize your Flask application and the best practices to follow.

Basic Flask Project Structure

At its simplest, a Flask application might only need a single file (e.g., app.py). However, as your application grows, you'll want to break it down into multiple files and directories for better organization. Here's a common structure for a larger Flask project:

plaintext

CopyEdit

```
your_project/
│
├── app/
│   ├── __init__.py
│   ├── routes.py
│   ├── models.py
```

```
|      └── config.py
|
├── venv/  # Your virtual environment
├── requirements.txt
└── run.py  # Entry point to start the Flask app
```

Explanation of the Structure

- **app/**: This directory contains the core functionality of your Flask app. It's typically where you put your models, routes, and configuration files.
  - **__init__.py**: Initializes your Flask application and sets up necessary extensions (such as the database or authentication system).
  - **routes.py**: Contains the route definitions for your app. You may create multiple files to organize routes based on their functionality (e.g., auth_routes.py or user_routes.py).
  - **models.py**: Defines the data models for your app, including database schemas and relationships.
  - **config.py**: Stores configuration settings such as database URLs, secret keys, and environment settings.
- **run.py**: This is the entry point for starting the Flask application. It imports the app from the app/ directory and runs it.
- **requirements.txt**: A file that lists all the Python packages required for the project. You can generate it by running pip freeze > requirements.txt.

Best Practices for Flask Development

- **Use Blueprints for Modular Code**: Blueprints allow you to organize your Flask app into reusable components. For example, you can create a blueprint for the user management system and another for handling product data.
- **Keep Configurations Separate**: Keep configuration variables (such as database credentials) in a separate config.py file. This will make it easier to switch between different environments (development, production, etc.).
- **Follow Naming Conventions**: Be consistent in naming your files, classes, and methods. This makes the code easier to read and maintain, especially when working in teams.

- **Use Environment Variables**: For sensitive information like API keys or passwords, use environment variables instead of hardcoding them into your app.
- **Version Your API**: When building an API, it's important to version it to ensure backward compatibility as your API evolves. You can do this by including the version in the URL (e.g., /api/v1/).
- **Implement Authentication and Authorization**: For APIs that require user interaction, implement authentication and authorization using Flask extensions like Flask-JWT or Flask-OAuth. Always secure sensitive routes and data.
- **Write Tests**: Flask has built-in support for unit testing. Always write tests for your routes, models, and other application logic to ensure reliability.

The structure of your Flask project should support scalability, readability, and maintainability. By following best practices and organizing your code properly, you ensure that your application remains clean and easy to work on as it grows.

Chapter 2: Building Your First API with Flask

2.1 Creating Your First Flask Application

Now that you've set up your environment and are familiar with the fundamentals of Flask, it's time to start building your first Flask application. Flask is designed to be simple, making it an excellent choice for beginners. Let's walk through the steps to create a basic Flask application that serves as the foundation for your first API.

Step 1: Install Flask

If you haven't already installed Flask, you can do so using Python's package manager, pip. Ensure that your virtual environment is activated, then run the following command:

```bash
CopyEdit
pip install Flask
```

This will download and install the latest version of Flask from the Python Package Index (PyPI).

Step 2: Create the Application File

In the root directory of your project, create a new file called app.py. This file will contain your Flask application code.

```python
CopyEdit
# app.py
from flask import Flask

# Initialize the Flask application
app = Flask(__name__)

# Define a route for the home page
```

```
@app.route('/')
def hello_world():
    return 'Hello, World!'

# Run the application
if __name__ == '__main__':
    app.run(debug=True)
```

Step 3: Breakdown of the Code

- **Importing Flask**: The first line imports the Flask class from the flask package. This is the core of any Flask application.
- **Creating the App Instance**: The Flask(__name__) line creates an instance of the Flask class. This object will be responsible for routing requests and managing the application.
- **Defining a Route**: The @app.route('/') decorator defines a route for the application. This route listens for incoming requests to the root URL (/), which is the homepage of your API.
- **Defining a View Function**: The function hello_world() is associated with the / route. This function returns a simple string message when the route is accessed.
- **Running the App**: The if __name__ == '__main__': block ensures that the application runs when the file is executed directly. The app.run(debug=True) command starts the Flask development server and enables debugging mode, which provides detailed error messages.

Step 4: Running the Flask Application

To run your Flask application, navigate to the directory containing app.py and execute the following command in your terminal:

bash
CopyEdit
```
python app.py
```

If the application runs successfully, Flask will start a local development server, usually on http://127.0.0.1:5000/. Open your web browser and navigate to this URL, and you should see the message "Hello, World!" displayed on the page.

Step 5: Making the First Step Toward an API

Now that you've created a basic Flask application, you're ready to start building your first API. Instead of returning just a simple string, you'll modify the application to return JSON data, which is the typical format for RESTful APIs.

Here's a simple modification to the hello_world route to return a JSON response:

```python
CopyEdit
# app.py
from flask import Flask, jsonify

app = Flask(__name__)

@app.route('/')
def hello_world():
    return jsonify(message="Hello, World!")

if __name__ == '__main__':
    app.run(debug=True)
```

By using jsonify, Flask converts your Python dictionary into a properly formatted JSON response. Now, when you access http://127.0.0.1:5000/, you'll receive the following JSON:

```json
CopyEdit
{
  "message": "Hello, World!"
}
```

This simple modification marks the beginning of your API development journey. You'll soon be adding more routes and complex functionality to your application.

2.2 Understanding HTTP Methods and Routes

In web development, HTTP (HyperText Transfer Protocol) is the foundation for communication between clients (browsers, apps, etc.) and servers. HTTP methods define the types of actions a client can request the server to perform on a resource. The key methods commonly used with RESTful APIs are **GET**, **POST**, **PUT**, **DELETE**, and **PATCH**.

In this section, we will dive deeper into how these HTTP methods are used in Flask to interact with resources, and how to define routes that respond to different methods.

Common HTTP Methods

- **GET**: Retrieves data from the server. It does not modify the resource.
- **POST**: Sends data to the server to create a new resource. It is typically used to submit forms or upload data.
- **PUT**: Replaces an existing resource on the server with new data.
- **DELETE**: Deletes a resource on the server.
- **PATCH**: Partially updates an existing resource on the server.

Each of these HTTP methods is used to perform CRUD operations (Create, Read, Update, Delete) on resources.

Defining Routes for Different Methods

In Flask, routes are defined using the @app.route() decorator, which maps a URL to a function. By default, Flask routes respond to the **GET** method. However, you can specify which methods a route should respond to by passing the methods argument to @app.route().

For example:

```python
CopyEdit
@app.route('/resource', methods=['GET'])
def get_resource():
    return jsonify({"message": "This is a GET request"})
```

This route will only respond to **GET** requests. If you send a **POST** request to the same URL, Flask will return a 405 Method Not Allowed error.

Here's how you can handle other HTTP methods like **POST**, **PUT**, and **DELETE** in Flask:

python
CopyEdit
```
@app.route('/resource', methods=['POST'])
def create_resource():
    data = request.get_json()  # Get JSON data from the client
    return jsonify({"message": "Resource created", "data": data}), 201

@app.route('/resource/<int:id>', methods=['PUT'])
def update_resource(id):
    data = request.get_json()
    return jsonify({"message": f"Resource {id} updated", "data": data})

@app.route('/resource/<int:id>', methods=['DELETE'])
def delete_resource(id):
    return jsonify({"message": f"Resource {id} deleted"}), 204
```

- **POST**: This route receives JSON data from the client, creates a resource, and returns the new data with a 201 Created status code.
- **PUT**: This route updates an existing resource. The id is passed in the URL, and the client sends new data to update the resource.
- **DELETE**: This route deletes the resource with the specified id. The server responds with a 204 No Content status code, indicating that the resource was successfully deleted.

Dynamic Routes and URL Parameters

Flask allows you to create dynamic routes that accept URL parameters. These parameters are passed to your view functions as arguments. For example:

python
CopyEdit
```
@app.route('/resource/<int:id>', methods=['GET'])
```

```
def get_resource_by_id(id):
    return jsonify({"message": f"Fetching resource {id}"})
```

In this example, <int:id> is a dynamic parameter that accepts an integer value. When a client sends a request to /resource/1, Flask will pass 1 as the id argument to the get_resource_by_id() function.

This flexibility makes Flask an ideal choice for developing RESTful APIs, where resources are often represented by dynamic URLs (e.g., /users/123, /posts/456).

2.3 Handling GET and POST Requests

GET and POST are the two most commonly used HTTP methods in web development. Understanding how to handle them in Flask is essential for building a functional API.

Handling GET Requests

A **GET** request is used to retrieve data from the server. It is the most common method used in RESTful APIs to fetch resources.

In Flask, GET requests are handled by default when no method is specified, as shown in the following example:

```python
CopyEdit
@app.route('/hello', methods=['GET'])
def hello():
    return jsonify({"message": "Hello, World!"})
```

This route responds to GET requests made to /hello. When a client sends a GET request, the server responds with a JSON message:

```json
CopyEdit
{
  "message": "Hello, World!"
}
```

20

If you want to fetch dynamic data, you can make use of URL parameters, as shown earlier. For example, to retrieve a specific resource by ID:

python
CopyEdit
```python
@app.route('/resource/<int:id>', methods=['GET'])
def get_resource_by_id(id):
    return jsonify({"message": f"Fetching resource with ID {id}"})
```

This route will return a response like:

json
CopyEdit
```json
{
  "message": "Fetching resource with ID 1"
}
```

Handling POST Requests

A **POST** request is used to send data to the server, typically to create a new resource. In Flask, you handle POST requests by specifying the POST method in the route decorator.

Here's how to handle a POST request that creates a new resource:

python
CopyEdit
```python
from flask import request

@app.route('/resource', methods=['POST'])
def create_resource():
    data = request.get_json()  # Get the JSON data sent by the client
    return jsonify({"message": "Resource created", "data": data}), 201
```

In this example, the create_resource() function retrieves the JSON data from the client using request.get_json(). The server then responds with the data and a 201 Created status code to indicate that the resource was successfully created.

To send a POST request, you can use tools like **Postman** or **curl**. For example, using **curl**, you can send a POST request to create a new resource:

bash
CopyEdit

```
curl -X POST http://127.0.0.1:5000/resource -H "Content-Type: application/json" -d
'{"name": "Example Resource"}'
```

The server will respond with the following JSON:

json
CopyEdit

```
{
  "message": "Resource created",
  "data": {"name": "Example Resource"}
}
```

Handling GET and POST requests is fundamental to building a RESTful API. GET requests allow clients to fetch data, while POST requests are used to send data to the server to create resources. Flask makes it easy to work with these methods, and the flexibility of its routing system allows you to easily design your API's endpoints to meet your application's needs.

In the next chapters, we'll continue to build on this knowledge, diving deeper into handling PUT, DELETE, and other HTTP methods, and exploring more advanced API design concepts.

2.4 Returning Data in JSON Format

When building a RESTful API, one of the most common ways to communicate data between the server and the client is using **JSON** (JavaScript Object Notation). JSON is lightweight, easy to read, and language-independent, making it a popular choice for data exchange in web APIs.

Flask, by default, returns responses in the form of plain text. However, Flask provides a simple and elegant way to return data in JSON format, which is the standard format for most modern APIs.

Why JSON?

JSON is a lightweight data-interchange format that's easy for both humans to read and write, and easy for machines to parse and generate. The primary reasons for using JSON in an API are:

1. **Human-Readable**: JSON is simple and easy to understand.
2. **Compact**: JSON data is minimal and concise compared to formats like XML.
3. **Interoperability**: JSON can be used across different programming languages and platforms.
4. **Compatibility**: JSON is natively supported by JavaScript and most modern programming languages.

How to Return Data in JSON Format in Flask

Flask provides the jsonify function, which is used to convert Python dictionaries into JSON-formatted responses. You don't need to manually convert Python objects into JSON strings. The jsonify function handles this automatically.

Here's an example of returning JSON data in a Flask route:

python

CopyEdit

```python
from flask import Flask, jsonify

app = Flask(__name__)

@app.route('/hello', methods=['GET'])

def hello_world():

  response = {

    'message': 'Hello, World!',

    'status': 'success'

  }

  return jsonify(response)
```

```python
if __name__ == '__main__':
    app.run(debug=True)
```

In this example:

- The hello_world() function returns a Python dictionary containing the key-value pairs for message and status.
- The jsonify() function takes this dictionary and converts it into a valid JSON response.

When a GET request is made to /hello, the server will respond with the following JSON:

json

CopyEdit

```json
{
    "message": "Hello, World!",
    "status": "success"
}
```

Handling Complex Data

For more complex data structures, jsonify() can handle nested objects as well. Here's an example of returning a list of resources in JSON format:

python

CopyEdit

```python
@app.route('/books', methods=['GET'])
def get_books():
    books = [
        {'id': 1, 'title': 'To Kill a Mockingbird', 'author': 'Harper Lee'},
```

24

```
    {'id': 2, 'title': '1984', 'author': 'George Orwell'},

    {'id': 3, 'title': 'The Great Gatsby', 'author': 'F. Scott Fitzgerald'}

    ]

    return jsonify(books)
```

This example returns a list of dictionaries (each representing a book), which Flask automatically converts to a JSON array. The response will look like this:

json

CopyEdit

```
[

  {

    "id": 1,

    "title": "To Kill a Mockingbird",

    "author": "Harper Lee"

  },

  {

    "id": 2,

    "title": "1984",

    "author": "George Orwell"

  },

  {

    "id": 3,
```

```
    "title": "The Great Gatsby",

    "author": "F. Scott Fitzgerald"

  }

]
```

Setting Proper HTTP Headers

In addition to returning the correct data, it's important to set the appropriate HTTP headers to indicate the type of data being returned. Flask does this automatically when you use jsonify. It sets the Content-Type header to application/json, which informs the client that the response body is in JSON format.

Here's how Flask automatically handles this for you:

python

CopyEdit

```
response = jsonify(data)

response.headers['Content-Type'] = 'application/json'

return response
```

But this is redundant since jsonify() already ensures that the response is properly formatted as JSON.

Error Handling and Returning JSON

It's important to properly handle errors and return informative responses in JSON format, especially in API development. You can return error messages in a consistent format using Flask's error handling mechanism.

For example:

python

CopyEdit

```python
@app.route('/resource/<int:id>', methods=['GET'])

def get_resource(id):

    resource = get_resource_from_database(id)

    if resource is None:

        return jsonify({'error': 'Resource not found'}), 404

    return jsonify(resource)
```

In this case, if the requested resource is not found in the database, the API will return a JSON object like this:

json

CopyEdit

```json
{

  "error": "Resource not found"

}
```

This consistency in error responses helps the client handle errors in a structured way.

2.5 Testing Your First API Using Postman

Once you've set up your first Flask API, it's crucial to test it to ensure that it works as expected. One of the most widely used tools for testing APIs is **Postman**. Postman
27

allows you to send HTTP requests to your API endpoints, inspect the responses, and ensure your application behaves correctly.

What is Postman?

Postman is a powerful tool that makes it easy to test APIs. It allows you to:

- Send HTTP requests to any endpoint.
- Inspect the response, including status codes, headers, and body.
- Test different HTTP methods (GET, POST, PUT, DELETE).
- Save and organize your API requests into collections for reuse.

Installing Postman

1. Go to the Postman website and download the Postman application for your operating system.
2. Install and open the application.

Making Your First API Request in Postman

Once Postman is installed and running, follow these steps to test the Flask API you've created:

Step 1: Set the Request Method to GET

To test the /hello endpoint that returns a simple "Hello, World!" message, first select the **GET** method in Postman.

Step 2: Enter the API URL

In the URL field, enter the following URL:

arduino

CopyEdit

http://127.0.0.1:5000/hello

This is the local address where Flask serves the application.

Step 3: Send the Request

Click the **Send** button in Postman. If everything is set up correctly, Postman will send a GET request to your Flask app, and you should see a response that contains the JSON data:

json

CopyEdit

```
{

  "message": "Hello, World!",

  "status": "success"

}
```

Testing POST Requests

Let's test a POST request to the /resource endpoint. For this, you'll need to add a request body containing the data you want to send.

Step 1: Set the Request Method to POST

In Postman, change the request method to **POST**.

Step 2: Enter the API URL

Enter the URL:

arduino

CopyEdit

```
http://127.0.0.1:5000/resource
```

Step 3: Add JSON Data in the Body

Switch to the **Body** tab in Postman, and select **raw**. Then, choose **JSON** from the dropdown. Add the following JSON data in the text area:

json

CopyEdit

```
{

  "name": "New Resource",

  "type": "Book"

}
```

Step 4: Send the Request

Click the **Send** button. Your Flask application will receive this data and process it. Assuming your route is correctly configured, you should receive a response like this:

json

CopyEdit

```
{

  "message": "Resource created",

  "data": {

    "name": "New Resource",

    "type": "Book"

  }

}
```

This shows that the POST request was successful, and the resource was created with the provided data.

Testing Other HTTP Methods

Postman allows you to test various HTTP methods such as PUT and DELETE by selecting the appropriate method from the dropdown. You can then follow similar steps to test those endpoints, making sure to include any necessary data in the body of the request (for PUT) or specify the resource ID in the URL (for DELETE).

Handling Response Status Codes

In addition to inspecting the response body, Postman shows the **HTTP status code** of the response. For example:

- **200 OK** indicates that the request was successful.
- **201 Created** indicates that a resource was successfully created.
- **400 Bad Request** indicates that the request was invalid (e.g., missing required parameters).
- **404 Not Found** indicates that the requested resource was not found.

You can use this information to validate that your API is working correctly.

Saving and Organizing Requests

Postman allows you to save individual requests and organize them into collections. This is especially useful when you're testing multiple endpoints or when you need to run tests repeatedly. To save a request, click the **Save** button, give it a name, and organize it into a collection.

Testing your Flask API using Postman ensures that your routes are functioning correctly and helps you catch errors early in the development process. Postman is an invaluable tool for debugging, testing, and validating your API, providing a user-friendly interface for making HTTP requests and inspecting responses. By using Postman to test your GET and POST requests, you'll be able to confidently build and refine your API, making sure it works as expected.

Chapter 3: Flask Fundamentals for API Development

3.1 Flask Application Structure

One of the reasons Flask is so popular is its flexibility and minimalism. Unlike heavier frameworks, Flask doesn't impose a strict project structure. However, this flexibility means that developers must define the structure of their application to ensure maintainability and scalability as their project grows.

A typical Flask application structure organizes files and directories in a way that separates concerns and allows for easier development, testing, and deployment. Let's look at how you can structure your Flask project, especially when building APIs.

Basic Structure of a Flask Application

At the most basic level, a Flask application could look something like this:

```
plaintext
CopyEdit
my_flask_app/

—— app.py          # Main application file
—— requirements.txt # Python package dependencies
—— venv/           # Virtual environment directory
—— run.py          # Entry point to start the Flask application
```

While this simple structure might work for small applications, it's important to note that as the project grows, splitting the application into multiple files and directories can make your code more organized and easier to manage.

Scalable Flask Application Structure

Here's an example of a more structured Flask application that is easier to scale and maintain as your project grows:

plaintext
CopyEdit

```
my_flask_app/
│
├── app/           # Main package
│   ├── __init__.py    # Initializes the Flask app
│   ├── routes.py      # Defines application routes
│   ├── models.py      # Contains data models (e.g., database schemas)
│   ├── config.py      # Configuration settings (database, API keys, etc.)
│   ├── services.py    # Business logic or helper functions
│   └── schemas.py     # Data validation (e.g., Marshmallow schemas)
│
├── venv/          # Virtual environment
├── requirements.txt   # Project dependencies
├── run.py         # Application entry point
└── instance/      # Config files for different environments (optional)
    └── config.py      # Config overrides for development/production
```

Let's break this structure down:

- **app/**: This directory contains the main Flask application code.
  - **__init__.py**: This file initializes the Flask application and sets up any required extensions, like the database or authentication mechanisms. It's common practice to create a factory function to initialize the app and extensions here, especially for testing purposes.
  - **routes.py**: This file defines the route handlers for the application. Routes map URLs to specific functions, and it's where you define your API endpoints.
  - **models.py**: If your API interacts with a database, this file holds the database models. Here, you define the structure of your data using an ORM like SQLAlchemy.
  - **config.py**: Holds all configuration settings, like the database URI, secret keys, and third-party API keys. By keeping configurations in one place,

33

you can easily switch between different environments (development, testing, production).

- ○ services.py: Sometimes called "business logic" or "helper functions," this file contains logic that doesn't belong in the route handler, like interacting with databases or performing calculations.
- ○ schemas.py: For validating and serializing data, especially in APIs, you might use a library like Marshmallow. This file will contain schema definitions that map your models to the desired JSON format.
- • instance/: This folder is used to hold instance-specific configurations, like a configuration file for development or production. This helps separate sensitive production credentials from your main code.

Best Practices for Flask Project Structure

- • **Modularize Your Code**: As your app grows, break it into logical components. For example, if your app has authentication and user management, you might separate the routes, models, and views related to users into a users/ module or package.

Use Blueprints: Flask supports **blueprints**, which allow you to define components of your app separately and then register them with the main Flask app. This helps organize routes and views related to specific parts of your application (e.g., authentication, users, products).

Example:

python

CopyEdit

```
from flask import Blueprint

auth_bp = Blueprint('auth', __name__)

@auth_bp.route('/login')
def login():
    return 'Login page'

@auth_bp.route('/signup')
def signup():
    return 'Signup page'

# In your main app, register the blueprint:
```

34

```
from app.auth import auth_bp
app.register_blueprint(auth_bp, url_prefix='/auth')
```

- **Testing**: Create a tests/ folder to store your test cases. Test individual modules, route handlers, and even specific functions. This keeps your codebase healthy and ensures everything functions as expected.

3.2 Routes, Views, and Flask Request Handling

In Flask, routes define the URLs where users can access resources in your application. These routes are mapped to specific functions, known as **view functions**, which process the request and return a response.

Understanding how routes work and how to handle requests properly is crucial for building robust APIs. Let's explore how routes and view functions work in Flask.

Defining Routes in Flask

Routes in Flask are defined using the @app.route() decorator. The decorator binds a URL to a function, so when that URL is visited by a client, the associated function is executed.

Here's an example of defining a simple route:

```python
CopyEdit
@app.route('/hello')
def hello_world():
    return 'Hello, World!'
```

In this example, when a GET request is made to /hello, the hello_world() function will be executed, and the client will receive the response: Hello, World!.

HTTP Methods in Routes

By default, routes in Flask handle **GET** requests. However, you can specify which HTTP methods a route should accept. This is useful for creating RESTful APIs where different HTTP methods (GET, POST, PUT, DELETE) are used to interact with resources.

To handle multiple HTTP methods, use the methods argument in the @app.route() decorator:

```python
CopyEdit
@app.route('/resource', methods=['GET'])
def get_resource():
    return 'Get Resource'

@app.route('/resource', methods=['POST'])
def create_resource():
    return 'Create Resource'
```

In this example:

- The GET /resource route retrieves a resource.
- The POST /resource route creates a new resource.

Flask also provides other HTTP methods such as **PUT**, **DELETE**, **PATCH**, which are commonly used in RESTful APIs for updating or deleting resources.

Request Handling

Flask allows you to easily retrieve data from the client's request. Depending on the type of request, you can access form data, query parameters, or JSON data sent by the client.

1. **Form Data**: If the client submits a form (like a POST request), you can access the form data using request.form:

```python
CopyEdit
from flask import request

@app.route('/submit', methods=['POST'])
def submit():
    username = request.form['username']
    return f"Hello, {username}!"
```

2. **Query Parameters**: For data sent in the URL as part of a query string (e.g., /search?query=flask), you can retrieve the values using request.args:
python
CopyEdit
@app.route('/search')

```
def search():
    query = request.args.get('query', '')
    return f"Search results for: {query}"
```

3. **JSON Data**: For APIs, you often work with JSON data. You can easily access JSON data in a POST request using request.get_json():
python
CopyEdit
from flask import request

```
@app.route('/json', methods=['POST'])
def json_data():
    data = request.get_json()  # Parse incoming JSON
    return jsonify(data)
```

Flask Response

The view function in Flask can return a simple string or more complex responses like JSON or HTML. The default response is plain text, but for APIs, it's common to return JSON.

You can return data in JSON format using the jsonify() function:

python
CopyEdit
from flask import jsonify

```
@app.route('/resource')
def resource():
    data = {'id': 1, 'name': 'Flask API'}
    return jsonify(data)
```

This will return a JSON response like:

json
CopyEdit
```
{
  "id": 1,
  "name": "Flask API"
}
```

Response Codes

Flask allows you to set the HTTP status code for responses. By default, Flask returns
200 OK for successful requests, but you can customize this as needed:

python
CopyEdit
```
from flask import jsonify

@app.route('/created', methods=['POST'])
def create_resource():
    data = {'message': 'Resource created'}
    return jsonify(data), 201  # 201 Created status code
```

3.3 Query Parameters and Path Variables

In Flask, you can pass dynamic values in URLs using **query parameters** and **path
variables**. Both allow the server to capture dynamic content from the URL and use it in
view functions.

Query Parameters

Query parameters are typically used in GET requests to filter, sort, or paginate
resources. These parameters are appended to the URL after the ? symbol, like so:
/search?query=flask&page=2.

To access query parameters in Flask, you use request.args. Here's an example:

python
CopyEdit
```
@app.route('/search')
def search():
    query = request.args.get('query')  # Access the 'query' parameter
    page = request.args.get('page', 1)  # Default to page 1 if not provided
    return f"Search results for: {query}, Page: {page}"
```

In this example, the query and page parameters are extracted from the URL. If the URL is /search?query=flask&page=2, the response will be:

yaml
CopyEdit
```
Search results for: flask, Page: 2
```

Path Variables

Path variables, or route parameters, allow you to capture values directly from the URL path. These are often used to access specific resources, such as /users/1 to access the user with ID 1.

In Flask, you define path variables using angle brackets < > in the route. For example:

python
CopyEdit
```
@app.route('/user/<int:id>')
def get_user(id):
    return f"User ID is {id}"
```

In this example, <int:id> captures an integer from the URL and passes it to the get_user() function. If the client accesses /user/123, the response will be:

pgsql
CopyEdit
```
User ID is 123
```

You can use various types for path variables:

- `<int:id>`: Captures an integer.
- `<string:name>`: Captures a string (the default type).
- `<float:price>`: Captures a floating-point number.

Using Both Query Parameters and Path Variables

You can combine query parameters and path variables to create more flexible routes. For example, let's say you want to retrieve a specific user by ID and include optional query parameters to filter or sort the results.

python
CopyEdit
```python
@app.route('/user/<int:id>')
def get_user(id):
    sort_by = request.args.get('sort', 'name')  # Default to sorting by name
    return f"User ID: {id}, Sorted by: {sort_by}"
```

If the URL is /user/123?sort=age, the response will be:

yaml
CopyEdit
```yaml
User ID: 123, Sorted by: age
```

Mastering routes, views, and request handling is essential for creating robust Flask applications and APIs. Understanding how to organize your Flask app and handle dynamic routes, HTTP methods, query parameters, and path variables will set a solid foundation for more complex API development. By following best practices for organizing your code and handling requests properly, you can build scalable and maintainable Flask APIs that interact seamlessly with client applications.

3.4 Flask Templates and Static Files

In Flask, you can serve dynamic content using **templates** and static files. Templates allow you to separate the logic of your application from the presentation layer, which is essential for keeping your codebase clean and maintainable. Static files, such as images, JavaScript, and CSS files, can be served to clients as they are without modification. This separation of concerns is particularly useful for creating web applications that rely on HTML for rendering data dynamically.

Flask Templates

Flask uses **Jinja2** as its templating engine. Jinja2 is a powerful and flexible template engine that allows you to embed Python-like expressions and logic into HTML files. Templates are stored in the templates/ directory and are rendered using Flask's render_template() function.

Creating Templates

1. **Directory Structure**

To use Flask templates, you'll need a templates/ directory in your project structure. Here's an example:

plaintext

CopyEdit

```
my_flask_app/
|
├── app/
|   ├── __init__.py
|   ├── routes.py
|   ├── templates/
|   |   ├── index.html
|   |   ├── about.html
|   ├── static/
|   |   ├── css/
|   |   ├── images/
|   |   └── js/
```

41

2. **Rendering Templates**

Here's a basic example of how to render a template in Flask:

python

CopyEdit

```python
from flask import Flask, render_template

app = Flask(__name__)

@app.route('/')
def home():
    return render_template('index.html', title="Home Page", message="Welcome to Flask!")

if __name__ == '__main__':
    app.run(debug=True)
```

In this example, when a user accesses the root route (/), Flask renders the index.html template and passes the variables title and message to it.

3. **Template Syntax**

Jinja2 templates use the following syntax for inserting variables and controlling logic:

- **Variable Substitution**: {{ variable_name }}
- **Control Structures** (like loops and conditionals):
  - For loops: {% for item in list %} ... {% endfor %}
  - Conditionals: {% if condition %} ... {% endif %}

Here's an example of a template that loops through a list:

html

CopyEdit

```html
<!-- index.html -->
```

```html
<!DOCTYPE html>
<html>
<head>
  <title>{{ title }}</title>
</head>
<body>
  <h1>{{ message }}</h1>
  <ul>
    {% for item in items %}
      <li>{{ item }}</li>
    {% endfor %}
  </ul>
</body>
</html>
```

In the view function, you can pass a list to be rendered:

python

CopyEdit

```python
@app.route('/')
def home():
    items = ['Item 1', 'Item 2', 'Item 3']
    return render_template('index.html', title="Home Page", message="Welcome to Flask!", items=items)
```

43

This will render a list of items on the webpage.

Static Files in Flask

Static files are files that do not change dynamically and can be served directly by the server. These include images, JavaScript files, and stylesheets (CSS). Flask serves static files from the static/ directory in your project.

Serving Static Files

1. **Directory Structure for Static Files**

In Flask, static files should be placed in the static/ directory:

plaintext

CopyEdit

```
my_flask_app/
├── app/
│   ├── static/
│   │   ├── css/
│   │   ├── js/
│   │   └── images/
```

Flask automatically maps requests to static/ to the /static/ URL.

2. **Referencing Static Files in Templates**

In your templates, you can reference static files using the url_for() function. For example, to link to a CSS file:

html

CopyEdit

```
<link rel="stylesheet" href="{{ url_for('static', filename='css/style.css') }}">
```

In this example, the url_for('static', filename='css/style.css') generates the URL for the CSS file located in the static/css/ directory.

Similarly, you can link to JavaScript files, images, and other static assets:

html

CopyEdit

```
<script src="{{ url_for('static', filename='js/app.js') }}"></script>

<img src="{{ url_for('static', filename='images/logo.png') }}" alt="Logo">
```

This allows Flask to handle static file serving efficiently.

3.5 Building API Endpoints with Flask

API endpoints are the backbone of a web application or service. They define the routes through which users or other applications interact with your data or business logic. Flask makes it easy to create RESTful API endpoints by mapping HTTP methods to route functions. In this section, we'll look at how to build API endpoints in Flask.

Defining API Endpoints

An API endpoint is essentially a route that performs a specific action (such as retrieving data or creating a resource) when a client sends an HTTP request. In Flask, you define these endpoints using the @app.route() decorator.

Here's an example of a basic API endpoint that responds to a GET request:

python

CopyEdit

```
@app.route('/api/resource', methods=['GET'])

def get_resource():

    data = {"id": 1, "name": "Flask API"}

    return jsonify(data)
```

In this example:

- The GET /api/resource endpoint returns a simple JSON object containing an id and name.
- The jsonify() function converts the Python dictionary into a JSON response.

Handling POST Requests

To create new resources, you typically use a POST request. In this case, the client sends data to the server, which creates a new resource and returns it.

python

CopyEdit

```
@app.route('/api/resource', methods=['POST'])

def create_resource():

    data = request.get_json()  # Get the data from the request body

    new_resource = {"id": 2, "name": data['name']}

    return jsonify(new_resource), 201  # Respond with the created resource and HTTP status 201
```

In this example:

- The POST /api/resource endpoint accepts JSON data from the client.
- The data is retrieved using request.get_json().
- The server creates a new resource and returns the newly created resource in the response body.

Path Variables in API Endpoints

You can use dynamic URL segments to capture variables in the URL path. This is useful for operations like retrieving or updating a specific resource based on its ID.

python

CopyEdit

```python
@app.route('/api/resource/<int:id>', methods=['GET'])

def get_resource_by_id(id):

    return jsonify({"id": id, "name": f"Resource {id}"})
```

In this example:

- The GET /api/resource/<int:id> endpoint dynamically captures the id from the URL.
- The value of id is passed to the get_resource_by_id() function, which then uses it to return a resource.

Combining Methods in Endpoints

You can combine multiple HTTP methods for the same endpoint to handle different types of requests. For example, you might want to use GET for retrieving a resource and DELETE for removing it:

python

CopyEdit

```python
@app.route('/api/resource/<int:id>', methods=['GET', 'DELETE'])

def manage_resource(id):

    if request.method == 'GET':

        return jsonify({"id": id, "name": f"Resource {id}"})

    elif request.method == 'DELETE':

        return jsonify({"message": f"Resource {id} deleted"}), 204
```

In this example:

- The GET /api/resource/<id> endpoint returns the resource with the specified ID.
- The DELETE /api/resource/<id> endpoint deletes the resource and returns a 204 No Content response.

3.6 Error Handling and Custom Error Pages

Error handling is an important part of API development. You want your users or clients to have clear, understandable messages when something goes wrong. Flask allows you to define custom error pages for common HTTP errors, such as **404 Not Found**, **500 Internal Server Error**, and others. You can also raise exceptions when something goes wrong in your application.

Default Error Handling in Flask

By default, Flask provides basic error handling for common HTTP errors. For example, if a route does not exist, Flask will return a 404 Not Found error, and if something goes wrong on the server, Flask will return a 500 Internal Server Error.

Custom Error Pages

You can create custom error pages for different HTTP errors by using the @app.errorhandler() decorator. This allows you to return a custom HTML page or JSON response instead of the default error message.

Here's an example of how to handle a 404 Not Found error:

python

CopyEdit

```
@app.errorhandler(404)

def not_found_error(error):

    return jsonify({"error": "Resource not found"}), 404
```

In this example:

- The @app.errorhandler(404) decorator tells Flask to call the not_found_error() function when a 404 Not Found error occurs.
- The function returns a JSON response with a descriptive error message.

Handling Other Errors

You can also handle other HTTP errors, such as 400 Bad Request, 500 Internal Server Error, and more:

python

CopyEdit

```python
@app.errorhandler(400)

def bad_request_error(error):

    return jsonify({"error": "Bad request"}), 400


@app.errorhandler(500)

def internal_server_error(error):

    return jsonify({"error": "Internal server error"}), 500
```

Raising Custom Exceptions

Flask allows you to raise custom exceptions in your application. For example, if a user tries to access a resource that doesn't exist, you can raise a 404 Not Found error explicitly:

python

CopyEdit

```python
from flask import abort
```

```
@app.route('/api/resource/<int:id>', methods=['GET'])

def get_resource_by_id(id):

    if id not in resources:

        abort(404, description="Resource not found")

    return jsonify({"id": id, "name": resources[id]})
```

In this example:

- If the resource with the specified id does not exist, Flask will automatically raise a 404 Not Found error.

Error handling is an essential part of building robust APIs. By providing clear, consistent error messages, you can help your users or clients understand what went wrong and how to fix it. Flask's built-in error handling, combined with custom error pages and exceptions, makes it easy to manage errors and deliver a better user experience.

By mastering these Flask fundamentals—templates, static files, building API endpoints, and handling errors—you can create clean, functional, and maintainable web applications that serve dynamic content and respond intelligently to user requests.

Chapter 4: Working with Databases in Flask

4.1 Introduction to Databases in Flask

In modern web development, most applications interact with a database to store and retrieve data. Databases serve as the foundation for handling persistent data—such as user information, product details, and transaction records—making them an essential component of any web application, including APIs built with Flask.

Flask, as a lightweight web framework, is designed to be flexible and allows you to integrate with a wide variety of databases. Whether you choose a **relational database** like MySQL, PostgreSQL, or SQLite, or a **NoSQL database** like MongoDB, Flask provides the tools and extensions necessary to work with your chosen data store.

In this chapter, we will focus on **relational databases**, which organize data into tables, rows, and columns, and the **SQLAlchemy** ORM (Object Relational Mapper) to interact with these databases in a more Pythonic way.

Relational vs NoSQL Databases

Before diving into using databases in Flask, it's important to understand the difference between relational and NoSQL databases.

- **Relational Databases**: These databases store data in structured tables. Each table has rows (records) and columns (fields). The structure of the data is strictly defined, and relationships between tables are managed through foreign keys. Examples include **MySQL**, **PostgreSQL**, and **SQLite**.
- **NoSQL Databases**: These databases store data in more flexible formats such as JSON, key-value pairs, or documents. They are often used for applications that require high scalability and handle semi-structured or unstructured data. Examples include **MongoDB** and **Redis**.

For Flask applications, **SQLAlchemy** provides a robust and flexible way to work with relational databases, while other extensions like **Flask-PyMongo** can help you integrate NoSQL databases.

Why Use SQLAlchemy with Flask?

SQLAlchemy is one of the most powerful and popular Object-Relational Mappers (ORMs) in Python. An ORM allows developers to interact with a relational database using Python objects, abstracting away the raw SQL queries. This makes database interactions more intuitive and Pythonic.

With SQLAlchemy, you can:

1. **Map Python Classes to Database Tables**: You define Python classes (models) that are automatically mapped to tables in the database.
2. **Query the Database Using Python**: Instead of writing raw SQL queries, you can use Python code to query and manipulate the database.
3. **Automate Table Creation and Schema Management**: SQLAlchemy can automatically create tables and manage schema changes using migrations.
4. **Ensure Database Compatibility**: SQLAlchemy supports various relational databases such as PostgreSQL, MySQL, and SQLite, allowing you to switch between different backends without changing much of your code.

In the following sections, we'll walk through setting up SQLAlchemy with Flask and using it to manage database interactions.

4.2 Using SQLAlchemy with Flask

SQLAlchemy is not part of Flask's core, but it can be easily integrated with Flask using the Flask-SQLAlchemy extension. This extension provides an easy-to-use interface for configuring and using SQLAlchemy in Flask applications.

Step 1: Installing Flask-SQLAlchemy

To get started with Flask and SQLAlchemy, you need to install the Flask-SQLAlchemy extension. Open your terminal and run:

```bash
CopyEdit
pip install Flask-SQLAlchemy
```

This will install both Flask and SQLAlchemy, along with the necessary dependencies for integration.

Step 2: Configuring Flask-SQLAlchemy

Once Flask-SQLAlchemy is installed, the next step is to configure the extension. To do this, you'll define the database URI (Uniform Resource Identifier) in your Flask application's configuration file.

Here's an example of how to configure a Flask application to use an SQLite database:

```python
CopyEdit
from flask import Flask
from flask_sqlalchemy import SQLAlchemy

app = Flask(__name__)

# Configure the database URI (here, using SQLite)
app.config['SQLALCHEMY_DATABASE_URI'] = 'sqlite:///example.db'
app.config['SQLALCHEMY_TRACK_MODIFICATIONS'] = False  # Disable modification tracking

# Initialize SQLAlchemy with the Flask app
db = SQLAlchemy(app)
```

In this example:

- **SQLALCHEMY_DATABASE_URI**: This configuration key defines the database connection string. In this case, we're using SQLite and storing the database file locally as example.db.
- **SQLALCHEMY_TRACK_MODIFICATIONS**: This option is set to False to disable Flask's modification tracking, which is unnecessary and could consume resources.

Step 3: Creating a Database Model

Now that we have Flask-SQLAlchemy set up, the next step is to define database models. A model represents a table in the database, and each attribute of the model represents a column in that table.

Here's an example of defining a simple User model:

python
CopyEdit
```python
class User(db.Model):
    id = db.Column(db.Integer, primary_key=True)
    username = db.Column(db.String(80), unique=True, nullable=False)
    email = db.Column(db.String(120), unique=True, nullable=False)

    def __repr__(self):
        return f"<User {self.username}>"
```

In this example:

- **db.Model**: This base class provided by Flask-SQLAlchemy is inherited by the User class. All models must inherit from db.Model.
- **id**: This is the primary key of the User table. It's defined as an integer and automatically generated by the database.
- **username and email**: These are columns in the User table. They're both strings and marked as unique to prevent duplicates. The nullable=False argument ensures that these columns cannot be empty.
- **__repr__**: This is a string representation of the object that will be used when printing a User object. It makes it easier to inspect instances of the model.

Step 4: Creating the Database

Once you've defined your models, you can create the corresponding tables in the database. To do this, you need to call the create_all() method provided by SQLAlchemy. This will generate the database tables based on the models you've defined.

python
CopyEdit
```python
# Create all tables in the database (if they don't already exist)
with app.app_context():
    db.create_all()
```

This will create an example.db SQLite database file and a User table if it doesn't already exist.

Step 5: Working with the Database

With SQLAlchemy configured and your model created, you can now perform basic database operations like adding, querying, updating, and deleting records.

1. **Inserting Data**:

To add a new user to the database, you can create a new instance of the User model and use SQLAlchemy's session to commit the changes:

```python
CopyEdit
# Create a new user
new_user = User(username="john_doe", email="john@example.com")

# Add the user to the session and commit the transaction
db.session.add(new_user)
db.session.commit()
```

2. **Querying Data**:

You can query the User table using SQLAlchemy's query interface:

```python
CopyEdit
# Get all users from the database
users = User.query.all()

# Query for a specific user by username
user = User.query.filter_by(username="john_doe").first()
```

3. **Updating Data**:

To update a record, simply modify the attributes of the object and commit the changes:

```python
CopyEdit
# Update a user's email
user.email = "new_email@example.com"
```

```
db.session.commit()
```

4. **Deleting Data**:

To delete a user from the database:

python
CopyEdit
```
# Delete a user
db.session.delete(user)
db.session.commit()
```

4.3 Setting Up Your Database Models

When working with Flask and SQLAlchemy, the process of defining and managing database models is crucial to the structure and functionality of your application. Models define how your data is stored in the database, and the relationships between different data entities (tables) in your application.

Defining Relationships Between Models

One of the most important features of SQLAlchemy is the ability to define relationships between tables (models). Flask-SQLAlchemy supports several types of relationships, including one-to-many, many-to-one, and many-to-many relationships.

1. **One-to-Many Relationship**

In a one-to-many relationship, one record in one table is related to multiple records in another table. For example, a **User** can have multiple **Posts**. Here's how you can define this relationship:

python
CopyEdit
```
class Post(db.Model):
    id = db.Column(db.Integer, primary_key=True)
    title = db.Column(db.String(120), nullable=False)
    body = db.Column(db.Text, nullable=False)
    user_id = db.Column(db.Integer, db.ForeignKey('user.id'), nullable=False)

    # Define the relationship between Post and User
```

```python
user = db.relationship('User', backref='posts', lazy=True)

def __repr__(self):
    return f"<Post {self.title}>"
```

In this example:

- **user_id** is a foreign key that references the id column of the User table.
- **db.relationship('User', backref='posts')**: This sets up the one-to-many relationship. It allows you to access a user's posts using user.posts, and it allows you to access the user for a specific post using post.user.

2. **Many-to-One Relationship**

A many-to-one relationship is simply the reverse of a one-to-many relationship. Each **Post** belongs to one **User**, and this relationship is defined in the Post model (as seen above).

3. **Many-to-Many Relationship**

A many-to-many relationship occurs when multiple records in one table can be related to multiple records in another table. For example, students and courses: A student can enroll in many courses, and a course can have many students. You would use an association table to represent this relationship:

python
CopyEdit
```python
course_student = db.Table('course_student',
    db.Column('course_id', db.Integer, db.ForeignKey('course.id'), primary_key=True),
    db.Column('student_id', db.Integer, db.ForeignKey('student.id'), primary_key=True)
)

class Course(db.Model):
    id = db.Column(db.Integer, primary_key=True)
    name = db.Column(db.String(100), nullable=False)
    students = db.relationship('Student', secondary=course_student, backref='courses')

class Student(db.Model):
    id = db.Column(db.Integer, primary_key=True)
```

```
name = db.Column(db.String(100), nullable=False)
```

In this example:

- The course_student table is the association table that links **students** to **courses**.
- The db.relationship function defines the many-to-many relationship between **Courses** and **Students**.

Model Validation and Constraints

SQLAlchemy allows you to add constraints and validation to your models to ensure that data meets certain criteria. For example:

- **Unique Constraints**: The unique=True option ensures that no two records in a column have the same value.
- **Not Null Constraints**: The nullable=False option ensures that a column cannot be empty.
- **Default Values**: You can set default values for columns using default=.

Example of adding constraints:

python
CopyEdit
```
class User(db.Model):
    id = db.Column(db.Integer, primary_key=True)
    username = db.Column(db.String(80), unique=True, nullable=False)
    email = db.Column(db.String(120), unique=True, nullable=False,
default="user@example.com")
```

In this example:

- The username and email columns must be unique and not null.
- The email column has a default value if no value is provided.

Working with databases in Flask is made simple and efficient through the use of SQLAlchemy. By defining models, creating relationships between them, and performing CRUD operations (Create, Read, Update, Delete), you can build robust applications that interact with databases seamlessly. Understanding how to configure your database models and set up relationships will form the backbone of your data-driven Flask application. With Flask-SQLAlchemy, you can ensure that your application handles data efficiently and maintains good performance as it scales.

4.4 Performing CRUD Operations

One of the fundamental tasks when working with databases in any web application is performing CRUD operations—Create, Read, Update, and Delete. These operations allow you to interact with the data in your database, whether it's adding new records, retrieving existing ones, updating them, or removing them.

In Flask, CRUD operations can be performed using **SQLAlchemy**. Let's walk through each of these operations with Flask-SQLAlchemy.

1. Create (Inserting Data into the Database)

To create new records in your database, you instantiate an object of the model class and then add it to the database session using db.session.add(). Once the object is added to the session, you need to commit the session to persist the changes to the database.

Here's an example of adding a new user:

python

CopyEdit

```
from flask import Flask

from flask_sqlalchemy import SQLAlchemy

app = Flask(__name__)

app.config['SQLALCHEMY_DATABASE_URI'] = 'sqlite:///example.db'

app.config['SQLALCHEMY_TRACK_MODIFICATIONS'] = False

db = SQLAlchemy(app)

class User(db.Model):

    id = db.Column(db.Integer, primary_key=True)
```

```
    username = db.Column(db.String(80), unique=True, nullable=False)

    email = db.Column(db.String(120), unique=True, nullable=False)

@app.route('/add_user')

def add_user():

    new_user = User(username="john_doe", email="john@example.com")

    db.session.add(new_user)

    db.session.commit()

    return f"User {new_user.username} added!"

if __name__ == '__main__':

    app.run(debug=True)
```

In this example:

- We create a new User object with the desired username and email.
- We add it to the session with db.session.add().
- Finally, db.session.commit() is called to commit the transaction and insert the record into the database.

2. Read (Querying Data from the Database)

Reading data from the database is done using SQLAlchemy's query interface. The most common method for querying is using query.all() to get all records or query.filter_by() for specific filters.

Example: Get all users:

python

CopyEdit

```
@app.route('/users')

def get_users():
```

```python
users = User.query.all()

return '<br>'.join([f"{user.username}: {user.email}" for user in users])
```

Here:

- User.query.all() retrieves all records from the User table.
- The function returns the usernames and emails of all users, separated by a line break.

To filter results by a specific attribute (like finding a user by email), you can use:

python

CopyEdit

```python
user = User.query.filter_by(email="john@example.com").first()
```

3. Update (Modifying Existing Data)

To update a record, first retrieve the object you want to modify, update its attributes, and then commit the changes to the session.

Example: Update a user's email:

python

CopyEdit

```python
@app.route('/update_user/<int:id>', methods=['GET'])

def update_user(id):

    user = User.query.get_or_404(id)  # Retrieve user by ID or return 404 if not found

    user.email = "new_email@example.com"  # Modify the email

    db.session.commit()

    return f"User {user.username}'s email updated to {user.email}"
```

In this example:

- User.query.get_or_404(id) retrieves the user with the specified id. If the user does not exist, it returns a 404 error.
- The email field is updated with a new value, and the change is committed to the database.

4. Delete (Removing Data from the Database)

Deleting records is straightforward in Flask-SQLAlchemy. First, you retrieve the object you wish to delete, then call db.session.delete() to mark it for deletion, and finally commit the changes.

Example: Delete a user:

python

CopyEdit

```
@app.route('/delete_user/<int:id>', methods=['GET'])

def delete_user(id):

    user = User.query.get_or_404(id)  # Retrieve user by ID or return 404 if not found

    db.session.delete(user)

    db.session.commit()

    return f"User {user.username} deleted!"
```

In this example:

- User.query.get_or_404(id) retrieves the user by ID.
- db.session.delete(user) marks the user object for deletion.
- db.session.commit() removes the record from the database.

These are the core CRUD operations you'll use frequently when building Flask applications. By utilizing SQLAlchemy's ORM functionality, you can abstract away the complexities of writing raw SQL queries and focus on working with Python objects instead.

62

4.5 Database Migrations with Flask-Migrate

As your application grows, so does your database schema. Adding new tables, modifying existing ones, and handling migrations (changes to the database schema) become essential tasks. **Flask-Migrate** is an extension that handles database migrations for Flask applications using **Alembic**, a database migration tool for SQLAlchemy.

Step 1: Installing Flask-Migrate

To get started, first install **Flask-Migrate** by running:

bash

CopyEdit

```
pip install Flask-Migrate
```

Step 2: Setting Up Flask-Migrate

Once Flask-Migrate is installed, you need to initialize it in your application. Here's how to do it:

python

CopyEdit

```python
from flask import Flask

from flask_sqlalchemy import SQLAlchemy

from flask_migrate import Migrate

app = Flask(__name__)

app.config['SQLALCHEMY_DATABASE_URI'] = 'sqlite:///example.db'

app.config['SQLALCHEMY_TRACK_MODIFICATIONS'] = False

db = SQLAlchemy(app)

migrate = Migrate(app, db)
```

Now, Migrate is initialized, and Flask-Migrate is ready to manage database migrations.

Step 3: Initializing Migration Scripts

With Flask-Migrate set up, you need to create migration scripts. These scripts contain the changes to the database schema that need to be applied.

To generate an initial migration, use the following commands:

bash

CopyEdit

```
flask db init        # Initializes the migration directory

flask db migrate     # Creates a migration script based on changes in models

flask db upgrade     # Applies the migration to the database
```

The flask db init command creates a migrations/ directory, which contains the migration scripts. flask db migrate generates a script based on the changes to your models, and flask db upgrade applies those changes to the database.

Step 4: Making and Applying Future Migrations

As your models evolve, you may need to make additional changes. For example, if you add a new column or modify a table structure, you can use the following commands to generate and apply new migrations:

bash

CopyEdit

```
flask db migrate     # Detects changes in your models and generates a new migration

flask db upgrade     # Applies the new migration to the database
```

Step 5: Downgrading the Database

If something goes wrong or you need to roll back a migration, you can use the following command to downgrade to a previous version:

bash

CopyEdit

```
flask db downgrade   # Rolls back to the previous migration version
```

With Flask-Migrate, you can manage complex schema changes while keeping track of your database version history and making migrations easy to apply across different environments (development, testing, production).

4.6 Handling Database Relationships

In Flask-SQLAlchemy, you can define relationships between tables using **foreign keys** and **relationship attributes**. These relationships allow you to model the relationships between different entities in your application.

One-to-Many Relationship

In a one-to-many relationship, one record in one table is associated with multiple records in another table. For example, a **User** can have many **Posts**.

To model this relationship:

python

CopyEdit

```
class User(db.Model):

    id = db.Column(db.Integer, primary_key=True)

    username = db.Column(db.String(80), unique=True, nullable=False)

    posts = db.relationship('Post', backref='author', lazy=True)

class Post(db.Model):
```

65

```
id = db.Column(db.Integer, primary_key=True)

title = db.Column(db.String(120), nullable=False)

body = db.Column(db.Text, nullable=False)

user_id = db.Column(db.Integer, db.ForeignKey('user.id'), nullable=False)
```

In this example:

- **db.relationship()** is used to define the one-to-many relationship between User and Post.
- **backref='author'** allows access to the user from a post object using post.author.
- **user_id** in the Post model is a foreign key that references the id of the User model.

Many-to-Many Relationship

In a many-to-many relationship, multiple records in one table are related to multiple records in another table. For example, students can enroll in many courses, and each course can have many students.

Here's how to define a many-to-many relationship using an **association table**:

python

CopyEdit

```
course_student = db.Table('course_student',

    db.Column('course_id', db.Integer, db.ForeignKey('course.id'), primary_key=True),

    db.Column('student_id', db.Integer, db.ForeignKey('student.id'), primary_key=True)

)

class Course(db.Model):

    id = db.Column(db.Integer, primary_key=True)

    name = db.Column(db.String(100), nullable=False)
```

```
    students = db.relationship('Student', secondary=course_student, backref='courses')

class Student(db.Model):

    id = db.Column(db.Integer, primary_key=True)

    name = db.Column(db.String(100), nullable=False)
```

In this example:

- **course_student** is the association table that links **students** and **courses**.
- **db.relationship()** defines the many-to-many relationship, with the secondary argument pointing to the association table.

One-to-One Relationship

In a one-to-one relationship, each record in one table is related to one record in another table. For example, a **User** can have one **Profile**.

python

CopyEdit

```
class Profile(db.Model):

    id = db.Column(db.Integer, primary_key=True)

    bio = db.Column(db.String(500))

    user_id = db.Column(db.Integer, db.ForeignKey('user.id'))

    user = db.relationship('User', backref='profile', uselist=False)
```

In this example:

- **user_id** is a foreign key that references the User model.
- **db.relationship(..., uselist=False)** ensures that each user has only one profile.

67

4.7 Introduction to NoSQL: Using MongoDB with Flask

While SQL databases are excellent for structured, relational data, some applications require a more flexible approach to data storage. **NoSQL databases** are well-suited for such use cases. NoSQL databases (like MongoDB) store data in formats like JSON, and they are particularly useful when dealing with unstructured or semi-structured data.

What is MongoDB?

MongoDB is one of the most popular NoSQL databases. It stores data as **documents** in collections (analogous to tables in relational databases). Documents are JSON-like structures with key-value pairs, allowing for highly flexible data models.

Using MongoDB with Flask

To use MongoDB in Flask, you'll need to install **Flask-PyMongo**, an extension that simplifies the integration of Flask with MongoDB.

bash

CopyEdit

```
pip install Flask-PyMongo
```

Setting Up Flask with MongoDB

Here's how you can configure Flask to work with MongoDB using Flask-PyMongo:

python

CopyEdit

```
from flask import Flask

from flask_pymongo import PyMongo


app = Flask(__name__)

app.config["MONGO_URI"] = "mongodb://localhost:27017/myDatabase"
```

```python
mongo = PyMongo(app)


@app.route('/')

def index():

    # Access a collection in the MongoDB database

    users = mongo.db.users.find()

    return f"Found {users.count()} users."


if __name__ == '__main__':

    app.run(debug=True)
```

In this example:

- **MONGO_URI** configures the connection to the MongoDB server.
- **mongo.db** allows access to the database, where you can query collections like users in this case.

Performing CRUD Operations with MongoDB

CRUD operations in MongoDB are very straightforward. Let's go through each operation.

1. **Create**: Insert a document into a collection:

python

CopyEdit

```
mongo.db.users.insert_one({"name": "John Doe", "email": "john@example.com"})
```

2. **Read**: Query documents from a collection:

python

CopyEdit

```
user = mongo.db.users.find_one({"name": "John Doe"})
```

3. **Update**: Update a document in a collection:

python

CopyEdit

```
mongo.db.users.update_one({"name": "John Doe"}, {"$set": {"email": "newemail@example.com"}})
```

4. **Delete**: Delete a document from a collection:

python

CopyEdit

```
mongo.db.users.delete_one({"name": "John Doe"})
```

MongoDB is an excellent choice for applications that require flexible schema designs or handle unstructured data. By using **Flask-PyMongo**, you can easily integrate MongoDB into your Flask application and perform standard CRUD operations. Understanding when to use SQL versus NoSQL databases is critical in choosing the right data storage solution for your application.

Chapter 5: Building RESTful APIs with Flask

5.1 What Makes an API RESTful?

A **RESTful API** follows the principles of **Representational State Transfer (REST)**, an architectural style that defines a set of constraints to enable scalable and stateless communication between a client and a server. REST has become the de facto standard for building APIs due to its simplicity, scalability, and performance.

For an API to be considered RESTful, it must adhere to the following constraints:

1. Statelessness

In REST, each request from a client to the server must contain all the necessary information for the server to understand and process the request. This means that the server does not store any information about previous client requests. Every request is independent, and the server does not rely on any stored session information. This helps scale applications by allowing the server to handle each request without any context about prior requests.

For example, if a client wants to access a user's data, the client should include all required information (such as authentication tokens) in the request, and the server processes it as if it's a new, independent request.

2. Client-Server Architecture

A RESTful API follows a **client-server architecture**, where the client (typically a web or mobile application) and the server are separate entities that communicate over a network. The client is responsible for handling the user interface and user interactions, while the server manages the application logic, data storage, and processing. This separation allows for better modularity and scalability, as each part can evolve independently.

3. Uniform Interface

A RESTful API must have a **uniform interface,** which ensures that the API is easy to use and understand. This means that the API should follow consistent conventions for naming, structuring endpoints, and using HTTP methods. For example:

- **GET** requests retrieve data.
- **POST** requests create new resources.
- **PUT** requests update existing resources.
- **DELETE** requests remove resources.

This uniformity allows developers to learn the API quickly, as the interactions with the server become predictable.

4. Resource-Based

In REST, the concept of **resources** is central. Resources refer to the objects or entities that the API is designed to manage (such as users, products, or posts). Resources are represented as URIs (Uniform Resource Identifiers), and the server responds to HTTP requests with representations of those resources, typically in **JSON** or **XML** format.

For example:

- /users could represent a collection of user records.
- /users/1 could represent a specific user with ID 1.

Each resource is identified by a unique URL, and clients interact with these resources through standard HTTP methods (GET, POST, PUT, DELETE).

5. Representation of Resources

A RESTful API does not directly expose its underlying database models. Instead, it exposes **representations** of resources, typically in JSON format. The representation includes the resource's data and may also include related resources (links to other resources).

For example, the representation of a user might look like this:

json
CopyEdit
{

73

```
"id": 1,
"username": "john_doe",
"email": "john@example.com",
"_links": {
  "self": "/users/1",
  "posts": "/users/1/posts"
}
}
```

In this example, the "_links" section provides links to other resources related to the user.

6. Stateless Communication

In REST, every request made by the client to the server is treated as an independent, stateless transaction. This means the server does not store any session data between requests. If a client wants to interact with the server, it must send all the necessary information (such as authentication data) with each request.

For example, when a client makes a request to access a protected resource, the client must include the necessary authentication token in the request header. The server does not remember that the client was authenticated in previous requests; each request is self-contained.

7. Caching

REST allows for caching of responses, improving performance and reducing server load. Responses from the server can be marked as cacheable or non-cacheable, depending on the use case. By caching responses, clients can reuse previously fetched data without needing to make another request to the server.

For example, when a resource is unlikely to change (like a list of countries), the response can be cached, saving time and resources for subsequent requests.

8. Layered System

REST allows for a **layered system** where intermediaries, such as load balancers, proxies, and firewalls, can be placed between the client and server. These intermediaries can perform various tasks such as load balancing, caching, and security checks without the client knowing. This layered approach enables scalability and modularity.

Summary of REST Principles

To summarize, an API is RESTful if it adheres to the following principles:

- Statelessness
- Client-server architecture
- Uniform interface
- Resource-based design
- Representation of resources (usually in JSON format)
- Stateless communication
- Caching for performance
- Layered system architecture

By adhering to these principles, you create an API that is scalable, modular, and easy to maintain.

5.2 Structuring RESTful Routes

Structuring routes is a critical part of building RESTful APIs. Routes define how clients interact with resources and ensure that the API is intuitive and easy to use. In Flask, routes are defined using the @app.route() decorator, which maps URLs to functions that handle the client's request.

When structuring RESTful routes, it's essential to follow some best practices to ensure consistency and clarity.

1. Use Nouns for Resources

In RESTful APIs, routes typically represent resources and actions. **Resources** should be represented using **nouns** (such as /users, /products, /posts), while **actions** should be inferred from the HTTP methods used (GET, POST, PUT, DELETE). This helps create routes that are semantic and easy to understand.

For example:

- **GET /users**: Retrieves a list of users.
- **POST /users**: Creates a new user.
- **GET /users/{id}**: Retrieves the details of a specific user.
- **PUT /users/{id}**: Updates the details of a specific user.
- **DELETE /users/{id}**: Deletes a specific user.

2. Use HTTP Methods to Define Actions

In a RESTful API, HTTP methods define the action performed on a resource. Here's how you can structure your routes based on the actions:

- **GET**: Retrieve a resource (or list of resources).
- **POST**: Create a new resource.
- **PUT**: Update an existing resource.
- **DELETE**: Remove a resource.

Here's an example of how routes map to HTTP methods:

```python
CopyEdit
@app.route('/users', methods=['GET'])
def get_users():
    # Fetch all users from the database
    pass

@app.route('/users', methods=['POST'])
def create_user():
    # Create a new user
    pass

@app.route('/users/<int:id>', methods=['GET'])
def get_user(id):
    # Fetch a specific user by ID
    pass

@app.route('/users/<int:id>', methods=['PUT'])
def update_user(id):
    # Update the details of a specific user
    pass

@app.route('/users/<int:id>', methods=['DELETE'])
def delete_user(id):
    # Delete a user by ID
    pass
```

In this example:

- The route /users maps to GET for retrieving users and POST for creating users.
- The route /users/<id> maps to GET for retrieving a specific user, PUT for updating, and DELETE for deleting the user.

3. Use Plural Nouns for Collections

It's a common convention in RESTful APIs to use **plural nouns** for collection resources and **singular nouns** for individual resources. For example:

- **GET /users**: Retrieves all users (a collection).
- **GET /users/{id}**: Retrieves a specific user (an individual resource).

This helps distinguish between requests for a collection and requests for a specific resource.

4. Nesting Routes for Subresources

For hierarchical relationships, it's common to nest routes to represent subresources. For example, if a **User** has many **Posts**, the following routes would make sense:

- **GET /users/{id}/posts**: Retrieves all posts for a specific user.
- **POST /users/{id}/posts**: Creates a new post for a specific user.
- **GET /users/{id}/posts/{post_id}**: Retrieves a specific post by its ID for a specific user.
- **PUT /users/{id}/posts/{post_id}**: Updates a specific post by its ID for a specific user.
- **DELETE /users/{id}/posts/{post_id}**: Deletes a specific post for a user.

python
CopyEdit
```python
@app.route('/users/<int:id>/posts', methods=['GET'])
def get_user_posts(id):
    # Fetch posts for the specified user
    pass

@app.route('/users/<int:id>/posts', methods=['POST'])
def create_post(id):
    # Create a new post for the specified user
```

```
    pass
@app.route('/users/<int:id>/posts/<int:post_id>', methods=['GET'])
def get_post(id, post_id):
    # Fetch a specific post for the user
    pass

@app.route('/users/<int:id>/posts/<int:post_id>', methods=['PUT'])
def update_post(id, post_id):
    # Update a specific post for the user
    pass

@app.route('/users/<int:id>/posts/<int:post_id>', methods=['DELETE'])
def delete_post(id, post_id):
    # Delete a specific post for the user
    pass
```

By nesting routes, you can express the relationship between resources clearly in the URL.

5.3 Managing HTTP Response Codes and Status Messages

Managing **HTTP response codes** and **status messages** is crucial for creating a RESTful API that is informative and easy to debug. HTTP response codes indicate whether a request was successful, and status messages provide additional information about the request's result.

1. Common HTTP Response Codes

Here are some commonly used HTTP status codes in RESTful APIs:

- **200 OK**: The request was successful, and the response body contains the requested data.
- **201 Created**: The request was successful, and a new resource was created.
- **204 No Content**: The request was successful, but there is no content to return (often used in DELETE requests).
- **400 Bad Request**: The request was invalid or malformed (e.g., missing required parameters).
- **401 Unauthorized**: The client must authenticate before accessing the resource.

- **404 Not Found**: The requested resource was not found.
- **405 Method Not Allowed**: The HTTP method is not supported for the requested resource.
- **500 Internal Server Error**: The server encountered an error while processing the request.

2. Flask Response Codes

Flask allows you to return custom response codes and messages in your API. By using jsonify() for JSON responses and returning a tuple with the data and status code, you can set the appropriate status code for each response.

Example:

```python
CopyEdit
from flask import jsonify

@app.route('/users', methods=['GET'])
def get_users():
    users = [{'id': 1, 'username': 'john_doe'}]
    return jsonify(users), 200  # 200 OK status
```

In this example, the API returns a list of users and a 200 OK status code.

3. Handling Errors and Custom Status Codes

When errors occur, it's important to return appropriate error codes and messages. Flask allows you to customize error handling using the @app.errorhandler() decorator.

Example of returning a custom error message and status code:

```python
CopyEdit
@app.route('/user/<int:id>', methods=['GET'])
def get_user(id):
    user = User.query.get(id)
    if user is None:
        return jsonify({"error": "User not found"}), 404  # 404 Not Found
```

```
return jsonify({"id": user.id, "username": user.username}), 200
```

In this example:

- If the user is not found, the API returns a 404 Not Found error with a custom error message.

4. Providing Detailed Error Responses

It's also a good practice to provide detailed error responses, including information about the error. For example, when validation fails or there is a malformed request:

python
CopyEdit
```
@app.route('/user', methods=['POST'])
def create_user():
    if not request.json or not 'username' in request.json:
        return jsonify({"error": "Bad Request", "message": "Username is required"}), 400
    username = request.json['username']
    user = User(username=username)
    db.session.add(user)
    db.session.commit()
    return jsonify({"id": user.id, "username": user.username}), 201
```

In this example:

- If the username is missing in the request, the API returns a 400 Bad Request status with a detailed error message.

Building RESTful APIs with Flask involves structuring routes, handling HTTP methods appropriately, and managing status codes and error responses. By adhering to RESTful principles and using Flask's routing, request handling, and response capabilities, you can build powerful, scalable, and user-friendly APIs. Properly managing HTTP response codes ensures that your API clients can easily understand the outcome of their requests and handle errors effectively.

5.4 Advanced Routing with Flask-RESTful

Flask-RESTful is an extension for Flask that adds support for building REST APIs in a more structured and organized way. It simplifies routing, handling request parsing, and generating responses by providing tools to create resources and manage HTTP methods more intuitively. Flask-RESTful abstracts some of the more repetitive tasks of building APIs, allowing developers to focus on their application's logic.

Setting Up Flask-RESTful

First, to get started with **Flask-RESTful**, you'll need to install the extension. You can do this with pip:

bash

CopyEdit

```
pip install flask-restful
```

Once installed, integrate it into your Flask application as follows:

python

CopyEdit

```
from flask import Flask
from flask_restful import Api, Resource


app = Flask(__name__)
api = Api(app)
```

```
;.L.class HelloWorld(Resource):

    def get(self):

        return {'message': 'Hello, World!'}


api.add_resource(HelloWorld, '/')


if __name__ == '__main__':

    app.run(debug=True)
```

In this example:

- We import the Api class from flask_restful, which sets up the Flask-RESTful API.
- Resource is a base class that provides a simple way to define resources that respond to HTTP methods (GET, POST, etc.).
- We create a HelloWorld class that inherits from Resource and implement a get() method to handle GET requests to the root URL (/).
- Finally, we add the resource to the API with api.add_resource(HelloWorld, '/'), mapping the HelloWorld resource to the / endpoint.

Advanced Routing with Flask-RESTful

Flask-RESTful allows you to define complex routing scenarios with ease. It offers the following features for advanced routing:

Parameterized Routes: Flask-RESTful supports parameterized routes in a manner that is more convenient than Flask's default routing.
For example:
python
CopyEdit
```
class User(Resource):
```

```python
def get(self, user_id):

    # Fetch the user by ID

    return {'user_id': user_id}

api.add_resource(User, '/user/<int:user_id>')
```

- In this example, the <int:user_id> route parameter captures the user_id from the URL and passes it to the get() method as an argument.

Handling Multiple HTTP Methods: You can define multiple methods (such as GET, POST, PUT, DELETE) within a single resource class to handle different types of requests to the same route.
For example:
python
CopyEdit
```python
class User(Resource):

    def get(self, user_id):

        return {'message': f'Get user {user_id}'}


    def put(self, user_id):

        return {'message': f'Update user {user_id}'}


api.add_resource(User, '/user/<int:user_id>')
```

Nested Resources: If you need nested resources, Flask-RESTful makes it easy to define resources within resources. For example, a User may have Posts associated with it.
python
CopyEdit
```python
class Post(Resource):

    def get(self, post_id):
```
83

```python
        return {'message': f'Post {post_id}'}


class User(Resource):

    def get(self, user_id):

        return {'message': f'User {user_id}'}


api.add_resource(User, '/user/<int:user_id>')

api.add_resource(Post, '/user/<int:user_id>/post/<int:post_id>')
```

In this example:

- The User resource can be accessed using /user/{user_id}, and the Post resource is nested under the User resource at /user/{user_id}/post/{post_id}.

Handling Requests with Flask-RESTful

Flask-RESTful simplifies request handling by automatically parsing incoming JSON data and converting it into Python objects for easy manipulation. To handle POST or PUT requests with data, use the reqparse module (deprecated in Flask-RESTful version 0.3) or use request.get_json() for modern Flask applications.

python

CopyEdit

```python
from flask import request


class User(Resource):

    def post(self):

        data = request.get_json()  # Automatically parse JSON data
```

84

```
username = data['username']

email = data['email']

return {'message': f'User {username} with email {email} created'}, 201
```

Here, the post() method is designed to accept a JSON body, parse it, and return a response confirming the creation of a user.

Conclusion

Flask-RESTful is a powerful extension that streamlines the development of REST APIs in Flask by simplifying the creation of resources, handling request parsing, and managing responses. It is an essential tool for building structured, scalable, and maintainable APIs with Flask.

5.5 Pagination and Filtering Data

As your API grows and handles more data, it becomes essential to implement pagination and filtering to ensure that responses remain manageable and perform well. Pagination helps to break down large sets of data into smaller, more digestible chunks, and filtering allows clients to request only the data they are interested in.

Pagination in Flask

To implement pagination in your Flask API, you can use the query parameters in the URL to specify which page of results to return and how many items per page.

Here's an example of how to implement pagination:

python

CopyEdit

```
@app.route('/users')

def get_users():

    page = request.args.get('page', 1, type=int)  # Get the page number from the query
string
```

```
per_page = request.args.get('per_page', 10, type=int)  # Get the number of items per
page

users = User.query.paginate(page, per_page, False)  # Paginate the query result

return jsonify({

    'total': users.total,

    'pages': users.pages,

    'current_page': users.page,

    'users': [user.username for user in users.items]  # Return user data for the current
page

})
```

In this example:

- page and per_page are obtained from query parameters.
- User.query.paginate() is used to paginate the query results. It takes three arguments: the page number, the number of items per page, and whether to give a "false" value for the last argument to include or exclude the results after the given page.
- The response includes total pages, current page, total users, and the list of users for that page.

Example request: /users?page=2&per_page=5

Filtering Data

Filtering allows clients to query only the data they need, reducing unnecessary data transfer. You can implement filtering by adding query parameters for different fields.

Here's an example of how to filter users by their username:

python

CopyEdit

```
@app.route('/users')
def get_users():
    username = request.args.get('username')  # Get the username filter from query string
    if username:
        users = User.query.filter(User.username.like(f'%{username}%')).all()  # Filter users
    else:
        users = User.query.all()  # No filter, get all users


    return jsonify([user.username for user in users])
```

In this example:

- If the username query parameter is provided, the users are filtered by the username field using the like operator to match the query.
- If no filter is provided, all users are returned.

Example request: /users?username=john

Combining Pagination and Filtering

You can also combine pagination and filtering in the same route to offer more powerful query capabilities.

87

python

CopyEdit

```python
@app.route('/users')
def get_users():
    page = request.args.get('page', 1, type=int)
    per_page = request.args.get('per_page', 10, type=int)
    username = request.args.get('username')
    query = User.query
    if username:
        query = query.filter(User.username.like(f'%{username}%'))
        users = query.paginate(page, per_page, False)
    return jsonify({
        'total': users.total,
        'pages': users.pages,
        'current_page': users.page,
        'users': [user.username for user in users.items]
    })
```

Here, the route can be filtered by username and also support pagination with page and per_page query parameters.

5.6 Handling Authentication and Authorization

When building RESTful APIs, it is often necessary to protect endpoints and ensure that only authorized users can access certain resources. Authentication and authorization are the two main concepts that handle these security concerns:

- **Authentication** ensures that a user is who they say they are.
- **Authorization** ensures that an authenticated user has the necessary permissions to access a resource.

1. Authentication in Flask

One of the most common authentication methods for APIs is **JSON Web Tokens (JWT)**. JWT is a compact, URL-safe means of representing claims between two parties. In Flask, you can use the **PyJWT** library to handle JWT-based authentication.

Installing PyJWT:

bash

CopyEdit

```
pip install PyJWT
```

Here's an example of how to implement JWT authentication in Flask:

python

CopyEdit

```
import jwt
from flask import Flask, request, jsonify
from datetime import datetime, timedelta

app = Flask(__name__)
```

89

```python
app.config['SECRET_KEY'] = 'your_secret_key'

def generate_token(user_id):
    expiration = datetime.utcnow() + timedelta(hours=1)
    token = jwt.encode({'user_id': user_id, 'exp': expiration},
app.config['SECRET_KEY'], algorithm='HS256')
    return token


@app.route('/login', methods=['POST'])
def login():
    data = request.get_json()
    username = data.get('username')
    password = data.get('password')

    # Authenticate user (simple example)
    if username == 'admin' and password == 'password':
        token = generate_token(1)  # Generate JWT for the user
        return jsonify({'token': token})

    return jsonify({'message': 'Invalid credentials'}), 401


@app.route('/protected', methods=['GET'])
def protected():
```

```
token = request.headers.get('Authorization')

if not token:

    return jsonify({'message': 'Token is missing!'}), 401


try:

    decoded = jwt.decode(token, app.config['SECRET_KEY'], algorithms=['HS256'])

    return jsonify({'message': f'Hello User {decoded["user_id"]}'})

except jwt.ExpiredSignatureError:

    return jsonify({'message': 'Token has expired'}), 401

except jwt.InvalidTokenError:

    return jsonify({'message': 'Invalid token'}), 401
```

In this example:

- The generate_token() function creates a JWT that includes the user's ID and an expiration time.
- The /login endpoint authenticates the user (in a real-world scenario, you would check the username and password against a database) and returns a JWT.
- The /protected endpoint checks the Authorization header for a valid JWT and allows access to the protected resource if the token is valid.

2. Authorization in Flask

Once a user is authenticated, you can handle **authorization** by checking if the user has the right permissions to access a specific resource. You can use JWT claims to store the user's roles and check those roles before granting access to certain endpoints.

python

CopyEdit

```python
@app.route('/admin', methods=['GET'])
def admin():
    token = request.headers.get('Authorization')
    if not token:
        return jsonify({'message': 'Token is missing!'}), 401

    try:
        decoded = jwt.decode(token, app.config['SECRET_KEY'], algorithms=['HS256'])
        if decoded['role'] != 'admin':
            return jsonify({'message': 'You do not have access to this resource'}), 403
        return jsonify({'message': 'Welcome Admin!'})
    except jwt.ExpiredSignatureError:
        return jsonify({'message': 'Token has expired'}), 401
    except jwt.InvalidTokenError:
        return jsonify({'message': 'Invalid token'}), 401
```

In this example, the role is checked to ensure that the user has **admin** permissions before granting access to the /admin endpoint.

Authentication and authorization are essential for building secure RESTful APIs. Flask provides various options for implementing these mechanisms, including JWT, which offers a stateless solution for managing authentication and authorization. By combining

JWT-based authentication and role-based authorization, you can protect your API endpoints and ensure that only authorized users have access to sensitive resources.

Chapter 6: API Security Essentials

6.1 Protecting Your API with Authentication

Authentication is the cornerstone of any secure API. It ensures that only authorized users can access protected resources, preventing unauthorized access to sensitive data and operations. By verifying the identity of users, authentication serves as a gatekeeper, ensuring that the API is only used by legitimate clients.

Why is Authentication Important?

Without proper authentication, an API is open to abuse, such as:

- **Unauthorized access**: Users might gain access to private or restricted data.
- **Data breaches**: Sensitive data could be exposed or stolen by malicious actors.
- **Abuse of functionality**: Unauthorized users might perform operations (such as data modification or deletion) that they shouldn't be allowed to.

Authentication is critical in APIs that deal with user data, payments, sensitive personal information, or any other protected resource.

Common Authentication Methods

Basic Authentication Basic Authentication requires the client to send a username and password with every request. These credentials are encoded using Base64 and passed in the Authorization header.

Example:
bash
CopyEdit
Authorization: Basic <base64-encoded-username:password>

While this method is simple, it is not very secure because the credentials are sent in every request, and Base64 encoding is easily reversible.

Token-Based Authentication Token-based authentication is much more secure and commonly used in RESTful APIs. It involves generating a **token** after the user successfully logs in, which is then used for subsequent requests. Instead of sending username and password with every request, the client sends the token as part of the request header, usually in the Authorization header.

The token is typically a **JWT (JSON Web Token)** or a **Bearer Token**. For this, we'll explore **JWT** authentication in the next section.

Steps for Protecting Your API with Authentication

1. **Create a Login Endpoint**: The first step is to create an endpoint where the client can authenticate (login) and receive a token.

2. **Token Verification for Protected Routes**: For any protected routes, you will need to check if the token is valid. This process typically involves decoding the token and verifying its signature.

Example using Flask:

python
CopyEdit

```python
from flask import Flask, request, jsonify
from functools import wraps
import jwt

app = Flask(__name__)
app.config['SECRET_KEY'] = 'your_secret_key'

def token_required(f):
    @wraps(f)
    def decorated_function(*args, **kwargs):
        token = request.headers.get('Authorization')
        if not token:
            return jsonify({'message': 'Token is missing!'}), 401
        try:
            token = token.split(" ")[1]  # Extract token from Bearer
            jwt.decode(token, app.config['SECRET_KEY'], algorithms=['HS256'])
        except jwt.ExpiredSignatureError:
            return jsonify({'message': 'Token has expired'}), 401
        except jwt.InvalidTokenError:
            return jsonify({'message': 'Invalid token'}), 401
        return f(*args, **kwargs)
    return decorated_function

@app.route('/protected', methods=['GET'])
@token_required
```

```
def protected():
    return jsonify({'message': 'This is a protected route'})

if __name__ == '__main__':
    app.run(debug=True)
```

In this example:

- A token_required decorator is used to protect routes. It checks the Authorization header for a token, verifies its validity, and only allows access if the token is valid.
- The route /protected is now protected by token authentication.

Best Practices for Authentication

- **Use HTTPS**: Always use HTTPS to encrypt sensitive data, including usernames, passwords, and tokens, to prevent interception by attackers.
- **Use Short Expiry Times for Tokens**: For additional security, set short expiry times for tokens, forcing users to log in periodically.
- **Store Tokens Securely**: Never store tokens in places that can be easily accessed by attackers (e.g., browser local storage). Use secure HTTP-only cookies for client-side storage.
- **Use Strong Passwords**: Enforce strong password policies on your application to prevent weak password exploitation.

6.2 Using JWT (JSON Web Tokens) for API Security

JSON Web Tokens (JWT) is a popular standard for securely transmitting information between a client and a server. JWTs are used for **authentication** and **information exchange**. They are particularly useful for API security because they are compact, self-contained, and can be used for stateless authentication.

What is a JWT?

A JWT is a string consisting of three parts:

1. **Header**: Contains the metadata about the token, such as the signing algorithm (e.g., HS256).

2. **Payload**: Contains the claims, or the data you want to store (e.g., user ID, user role, expiration time). This data is base64-encoded but not encrypted.
3. **Signature**: A cryptographic signature that ensures the integrity of the token. It is created by signing the header and payload with a secret key.

A JWT typically looks like this:

plaintext
CopyEdit

eyJhbGciOiJIUzI1NiIsInR5cCI6IkpXVCJ9.eyJzdWIiOiIxMjM0NTY3ODkwIiwibmFtZSI6IkpvaG4gRG9lIiwiaWF0IjoxNTE2MjM5MDIyfQ.SflKxwRJSMeKKF2QT4fwpMeJf36POk6yJV_adQssw5c

How JWT Works

1. The client sends a request to the server with the user's credentials (username and password).
2. If the credentials are correct, the server generates a JWT that includes user-related data (such as user ID) and signs it with a secret key.
3. The JWT is sent back to the client, which stores it (usually in a secure cookie or in memory).
4. For subsequent requests, the client sends the JWT in the Authorization header.
5. The server verifies the JWT by checking the signature. If valid, it allows the request to proceed.

Implementing JWT Authentication in Flask

Let's implement JWT authentication in Flask for API security.

1. **Install PyJWT**:

bash
CopyEdit
pip install PyJWT

2. **Generate a JWT upon Successful Login**:

python

```
import jwt
from datetime import datetime, timedelta
from flask import Flask, jsonify, request

app = Flask(__name__)
app.config['SECRET_KEY'] = 'your_secret_key'

# Function to generate JWT
def generate_token(user_id):
    expiration = datetime.utcnow() + timedelta(hours=1)  # Token expires in 1 hour
    token = jwt.encode({'user_id': user_id, 'exp': expiration},
app.config['SECRET_KEY'], algorithm='HS256')
    return token

@app.route('/login', methods=['POST'])
def login():
    data = request.get_json()
    username = data.get('username')
    password = data.get('password')

    # In a real app, authenticate the user against a database
    if username == 'admin' and password == 'password':
        token = generate_token(1)  # Generate JWT for the authenticated user
        return jsonify({'token': token})

    return jsonify({'message': 'Invalid credentials'}), 401

if __name__ == '__main__':
    app.run(debug=True)
```

In this example:

- The /login route authenticates the user and generates a JWT upon successful login.
- The generate_token() function creates a JWT that includes the user ID and an expiration time.

3. **Protecting Routes with JWT**:

python
CopyEdit
```python
from functools import wraps
from flask import request, jsonify

def token_required(f):
    @wraps(f)
    def decorated_function(*args, **kwargs):
        token = request.headers.get('Authorization')
        if not token:
            return jsonify({'message': 'Token is missing!'}), 401
        try:
            token = token.split(" ")[1]  # Extract token from Bearer
            jwt.decode(token, app.config['SECRET_KEY'], algorithms=['HS256'])
        except jwt.ExpiredSignatureError:
            return jsonify({'message': 'Token has expired'}), 401
        except jwt.InvalidTokenError:
            return jsonify({'message': 'Invalid token'}), 401
        return f(*args, **kwargs)
    return decorated_function

@app.route('/protected', methods=['GET'])
@token_required
def protected():
    return jsonify({'message': 'This is a protected route'})
```

In this example:

- The token_required decorator checks if the request has a valid JWT.
- If the token is valid, the user can access the /protected route; otherwise, a 401 Unauthorized error is returned.

Advantages of Using JWT

- **Stateless Authentication**: JWTs are self-contained, meaning the server does not need to maintain session information between requests.

- **Scalability**: Since JWTs are stored on the client side, they are easy to scale and distribute across multiple servers.
- **Security**: The signature ensures that the data in the JWT cannot be tampered with, and the token can include an expiration time to limit its lifespan.

Best Practices with JWT

- **Short Expiry Times**: Set short expiry times for JWTs to minimize the risk of an attacker using a stolen token.
- **Use HTTPS**: Always use HTTPS to prevent interception of tokens during transmission.
- **Store Tokens Securely**: Use secure storage mechanisms such as HTTP-only cookies to prevent client-side JavaScript from accessing the token.

6.3 Role-Based Access Control (RBAC) in Flask

Role-Based Access Control (RBAC) is a method of restricting access to resources based on the roles assigned to users. By implementing RBAC in your Flask API, you can ensure that different users have different levels of access to your API's resources. For example, administrators may have full access, while regular users may have limited permissions.

How RBAC Works

RBAC assigns roles to users, and each role has specific permissions or access levels. For example:

- **Admin**: Full access to all resources.
- **User**: Limited access, can only view certain data.
- **Guest**: Read-only access to public resources.

Implementing RBAC in Flask

You can implement RBAC by adding roles to your JWT tokens. The role is typically stored in the payload of the JWT, and routes are protected based on the role specified in the token.

1. Assigning Roles in JWT

When generating a JWT, you can include the role of the user in the payload:

python
CopyEdit
```
def generate_token(user_id, role):
    expiration = datetime.utcnow() + timedelta(hours=1)
    token = jwt.encode({'user_id': user_id, 'role': role, 'exp': expiration},
app.config['SECRET_KEY'], algorithm='HS256')
    return token
```

2. Protecting Routes Based on Roles

Once the token includes the role, you can protect routes by checking the role before granting access:

python
CopyEdit
```
def role_required(role):
    def decorator(f):
        @wraps(f)
        def decorated_function(*args, **kwargs):
            token = request.headers.get('Authorization')
            if not token:
                return jsonify({'message': 'Token is missing!'}), 401
            try:
                token = token.split(" ")[1]  # Extract token from Bearer
                decoded_token = jwt.decode(token, app.config['SECRET_KEY'],
algorithms=['HS256'])
                if decoded_token['role'] != role:
                    return jsonify({'message': 'You do not have permission to access this
resource'}), 403
            except jwt.ExpiredSignatureError:
                return jsonify({'message': 'Token has expired'}), 401
            except jwt.InvalidTokenError:
                return jsonify({'message': 'Invalid token'}), 401
            return f(*args, **kwargs)
```

```
        return decorated_function
    return decorator

@app.route('/admin', methods=['GET'])
@role_required('admin')
def admin_dashboard():
    return jsonify({'message': 'Welcome to the admin dashboard'})
```

In this example:

- The role_required decorator checks if the role of the user in the JWT matches the required role for the route.
- If the user is not authorized, a 403 Forbidden response is returned.

Best Practices for RBAC

- **Minimize Permissions**: Assign users the minimum permissions required to perform their tasks.
- **Regularly Review Roles**: Periodically review user roles and access permissions to ensure that users only have the necessary access.
- **Use RBAC for Sensitive Operations**: Use roles to protect sensitive data and critical operations such as deleting or modifying resources.

RBAC is a powerful way to manage user permissions and restrict access to resources based on user roles. By integrating RBAC into your Flask application, you can ensure that only authorized users have access to specific routes or actions, enhancing the security and usability of your API.

6.4 Preventing Common API Vulnerabilities (XSS, CSRF, SQL Injection)

Building secure APIs requires addressing various vulnerabilities that can be exploited by malicious actors. **Cross-Site Scripting (XSS)**, **Cross-Site Request Forgery (CSRF)**, and **SQL Injection** are some of the most common vulnerabilities that you should be aware of when developing APIs. Let's take a closer look at these vulnerabilities and how to prevent them.

1. Cross-Site Scripting (XSS)

Cross-Site Scripting (XSS) occurs when an attacker injects malicious scripts into web pages that are then executed by other users' browsers. This can allow attackers to steal session cookies, redirect users to malicious websites, or perform actions on behalf of the user without their consent.

Types of XSS:

- **Stored XSS**: The malicious script is stored on the server (e.g., in a database) and is served to users whenever they access the page.
- **Reflected XSS**: The malicious script is embedded in a URL and executed immediately when the URL is clicked.
- **DOM-based XSS**: The script is executed as a result of modifying the DOM (Document Object Model) in the browser via JavaScript.

Preventing XSS in Flask APIs:

- **Escape Data**: Always sanitize and escape user-generated content before rendering it on the front end. In Flask templates, use {{ data|escape }} to ensure that HTML tags are not rendered.
- **Content Security Policy (CSP)**: Implement a strict **Content Security Policy (CSP)** to mitigate the risk of XSS attacks. CSP allows you to specify trusted sources for JavaScript, which can prevent malicious scripts from running.
- **Use Safe Data Types**: Use JSON or other safe data formats that do not interpret HTML or JavaScript content.

python

CopyEdit

```
from flask import render_template_string

@app.route('/show_comment', methods=['GET'])

def show_comment():

    comment = request.args.get('comment')

    # Automatically escape HTML to prevent XSS
```

```
return render_template_string("<p>{{ comment }}</p>", comment=comment)
```

In this example, using Flask's template engine ensures that any data passed to the template is automatically escaped, preventing the injection of malicious scripts.

2. Cross-Site Request Forgery (CSRF)

Cross-Site Request Forgery (CSRF) is an attack where a user is tricked into submitting a malicious request (such as changing a password) on a website where they are authenticated, without their knowledge.

Preventing CSRF in Flask:

- **Use CSRF Tokens**: CSRF tokens are unique tokens generated by the server and sent to the client. The client must then include this token with every request that modifies data (such as POST, PUT, or DELETE requests). The server verifies that the token is valid and matches the one issued to the client, preventing unauthorized actions.
- **Flask-WTF**: Flask-WTF provides an easy way to manage CSRF protection in Flask applications.

Example of CSRF Protection:

python

CopyEdit

```python
from flask_wtf.csrf import CSRFProtect

app = Flask(__name__)
csrf = CSRFProtect(app)

@app.route('/submit_form', methods=['POST'])
def submit_form():
```

```
# Handle form submission

return "Form submitted successfully!"
```

In this example, Flask-WTF handles the CSRF protection automatically, ensuring that every POST request has a valid CSRF token.

3. SQL Injection

SQL Injection is a vulnerability where an attacker can manipulate an SQL query by injecting malicious SQL code into the query. This can lead to unauthorized access to data, deletion of records, or even full system compromise.

Preventing SQL Injection:

- **Use ORM (Object-Relational Mapping)**: An ORM like **SQLAlchemy** in Flask automatically escapes inputs to prevent SQL injection, as it doesn't directly generate raw SQL queries. This significantly reduces the risk of SQL injection.
- **Prepared Statements**: If you do need to execute raw SQL queries, use **prepared statements** or **parameterized queries**, which ensure that user inputs are treated as data rather than part of the SQL query.
- **Sanitize Inputs**: Always sanitize and validate user inputs before using them in SQL queries.

Example using SQLAlchemy (ORM-based approach):

python

CopyEdit

```
@app.route('/user/<int:user_id>')

def get_user(user_id):

    # SQLAlchemy prevents SQL injection by using parameterized queries

    user = User.query.filter_by(id=user_id).first()

    return jsonify({'username': user.username})
```

In this example, filter_by() uses parameterized queries, which means the user_id is never directly injected into the SQL query string, protecting the application from SQL injection.

Best Practices for Securing APIs

- **Sanitize All Inputs**: Ensure all user inputs (from URLs, form fields, or headers) are sanitized before processing.
- **Limit User Privileges**: Always implement the **principle of least privilege** by restricting access to sensitive actions and data. For example, only allow administrative users to delete data.
- **Error Handling**: Avoid exposing stack traces or detailed error messages to end-users. This could provide attackers with useful information on how to exploit your API.
- **Logging and Monitoring**: Regularly monitor and log suspicious activities. Having visibility into API requests can help detect and mitigate attacks early.

6.5 Securing Sensitive Data with SSL/TLS

Sensitive data, such as passwords, personal information, and payment details, must be transmitted securely between the client and the server. **SSL (Secure Sockets Layer)** and **TLS (Transport Layer Security)** are cryptographic protocols designed to secure communications over a network. Today, TLS is the standard, and SSL is considered deprecated.

When using **SSL/TLS**, data transmitted between the client and the server is encrypted, making it significantly more difficult for attackers to intercept and tamper with the data.

Why SSL/TLS is Important for API Security

- **Data Encryption**: SSL/TLS ensures that data is encrypted during transmission, protecting it from eavesdropping and man-in-the-middle (MITM) attacks.
- **Data Integrity**: SSL/TLS also verifies that the data sent and received has not been altered during transmission.
- **Authentication**: By using SSL/TLS certificates, clients can verify the identity of the server, preventing attackers from impersonating your API.

How SSL/TLS Works

SSL/TLS encrypts data using asymmetric encryption during the handshake and switches to symmetric encryption for the bulk data transfer. Here's a simplified view of how SSL/TLS works:

1. **Client Hello**: The client sends a "hello" message to the server, including its supported SSL/TLS versions and cipher suites.
2. **Server Hello**: The server responds with its chosen SSL/TLS version, cipher suite, and its **SSL/TLS certificate**.
3. **Certificate Validation**: The client validates the server's certificate to ensure it is issued by a trusted certificate authority (CA).
4. **Key Exchange**: The client and server exchange keys to establish a secure connection.
5. **Encrypted Communication**: Once the handshake is complete, all data transmitted between the client and server is encrypted using symmetric encryption.

Setting Up SSL/TLS for Flask

To secure your Flask API with SSL/TLS, you need to set up an SSL certificate and configure your server to use HTTPS.

Step 1: Obtain an SSL Certificate You can get an SSL certificate from a trusted **Certificate Authority (CA)** like Let's Encrypt (free) or purchase one from other providers. Alternatively, you can create a self-signed certificate for testing purposes (though this will not be trusted by browsers or clients without explicit configuration).

Step 2: Enable SSL/TLS in Flask

Once you have your SSL certificate, you can configure Flask to use HTTPS for secure communication.

Here's an example of how to run Flask with SSL enabled:

python

CopyEdit

```
from flask import Flask
```

107

```python
app = Flask(__name__)

@app.route('/')
def hello():
    return "Hello, Secure World!"

if __name__ == '__main__':
    # Provide paths to your SSL certificate and private key
    app.run(ssl_context=('cert.pem', 'key.pem'), debug=True)
```

In this example:

- cert.pem is your SSL certificate file.
- key.pem is your private key file.
- Flask will now serve content over HTTPS, securing communication between the client and server.

Best Practices for SSL/TLS in APIs

- **Use Strong Cipher Suites**: Ensure you are using strong cipher suites that are resistant to known cryptographic attacks.
- **Use HTTP Strict Transport Security (HSTS)**: HSTS forces clients to use HTTPS for all future requests to your domain, protecting against protocol downgrade attacks.
- **Regularly Renew SSL Certificates**: SSL certificates have expiration dates, and renewing them before expiration is crucial for maintaining secure communication.
- **Force HTTPS**: Redirect all HTTP traffic to HTTPS to ensure that all communication is encrypted.

Securing sensitive data is a critical part of API development. Using **SSL/TLS** ensures that data is encrypted during transmission and is protected from interception or tampering. Combined with other measures like **authentication, role-based access control (RBAC)**, and protections against common vulnerabilities like **XSS, CSRF**, and **SQL Injection**, you can build a robust and secure API. Regularly auditing and updating your security practices is essential to keeping your API safe from evolving threats.

Chapter 7: Testing and Debugging Flask APIs

7.1 Why Testing Matters in API Development

In any software development process, **testing** plays a critical role in ensuring that the application works as expected. This is especially true for APIs, where numerous requests, responses, and user interactions need to be properly validated. Testing ensures that your Flask API functions correctly, remains secure, and continues to deliver the expected results as it evolves.

Benefits of Testing APIs

1. **Detecting Bugs Early**: Writing tests for your API endpoints allows you to detect issues and bugs early in the development process. Catching bugs early helps prevent costly debugging later in the development cycle.
2. **Ensuring Code Quality**: Automated tests ensure that your code is well-structured and functions as intended. By testing individual components and API endpoints, you can be confident that the code is high quality and adheres to expected standards.
3. **API Contract Validation**: APIs serve as a contract between the client and the server. Testing helps validate that the API adheres to the expected behavior, returns correct status codes, and formats data properly.
4. **Facilitating Refactoring**: When refactoring code, tests act as a safety net. Since tests validate that the API still functions as expected, you can confidently make changes to the codebase without breaking functionality.
5. **Preventing Regression**: As APIs grow and evolve, regression testing ensures that new features or updates do not unintentionally break existing functionality. Testing helps maintain stability over time.
6. **Ensuring Reliability**: Automated tests provide continuous assurance that the API works as expected, reducing the likelihood of unexpected downtime or errors in production environments.

Types of Testing for APIs

1. **Unit Testing**: Unit tests focus on testing individual functions or methods in isolation. For API development, this often involves testing smaller units of the codebase, such as specific functions or routes.
2. **Integration Testing**: Integration tests validate that various components of the application (such as the database, third-party services, and API endpoints) work together seamlessly.
3. **Functional Testing**: Functional tests verify that the application performs the intended functions, typically by simulating end-to-end user interactions with the API.
4. **Performance Testing**: This type of testing ensures that the API can handle heavy loads and scale under demand. Tools like **Locust** or **JMeter** can be used for performance testing.
5. **Security Testing**: Security tests are used to identify vulnerabilities in the API, such as **SQL injection** or **Cross-Site Scripting (XSS)**. These tests help ensure that the API is secure from attacks.

The Importance of Automation

Automated testing is especially important for APIs due to the repetitive nature of API requests. Manually testing every API route and endpoint after each change can be time-consuming and prone to errors. Automated tests ensure that your tests are run every time code changes are made, ensuring that bugs are detected earlier and more efficiently.

Challenges of API Testing

1. **Simulating Real User Interactions**: APIs must be tested under various scenarios, such as invalid requests, high traffic, and edge cases. Testing must simulate real-world user interactions to ensure robustness.
2. **Handling External Dependencies**: APIs often interact with external services like databases, third-party APIs, or file systems. Mocking these dependencies for testing can be challenging but is necessary to ensure isolated unit tests.
3. **Managing Test Data**: Testing APIs often requires setting up and managing test data. Creating repeatable tests that work with different datasets is crucial for accurate testing.

By implementing testing early in the development cycle, you ensure that your Flask API is robust, reliable, and able to scale effectively in production environments.

7.2 Unit Testing with Pytest and Flask-Testing

Unit testing is the process of testing individual units or components of an application in isolation, usually by mocking external dependencies. In Flask, **Pytest** and **Flask-Testing** are two powerful tools commonly used for writing unit tests for Flask applications.

Why Pytest for Unit Testing?

Pytest is a testing framework for Python that makes it simple to write small, readable tests. It has several advantages:

- **Simplified syntax**: Pytest simplifies test writing by using regular Python functions, so there is no need to define test classes or methods.
- **Powerful fixtures**: Pytest's fixture system allows you to set up and tear down objects or resources that tests require.
- **Rich plugin system**: Pytest offers plugins for various use cases, such as mocking, code coverage, and integration with CI/CD tools.

Installing Pytest and Flask-Testing

To start using Pytest with Flask, you'll need to install pytest and Flask-Testing. Here's how you do it:

bash
CopyEdit

```
pip install pytest Flask-Testing
```

Setting Up a Simple Test for Flask API

Let's create a simple Flask application with one API endpoint and write unit tests using Pytest.

1. **Flask Application**

python
CopyEdit

```
from flask import Flask, jsonify

app = Flask(__name__)
```

```
@app.route('/greet', methods=['GET'])
def greet():
    return jsonify({"message": "Hello, World!"}), 200
```

2. Test for Flask API

Create a file called test_app.py to write unit tests for the API:

```python
CopyEdit
import pytest
from flask import Flask
from app import app  # Assuming app.py contains the Flask app

@pytest.fixture
def client():
    with app.test_client() as client:
        yield client

def test_greet(client):
    response = client.get('/greet')
    assert response.status_code == 200
    assert response.json == {"message": "Hello, World!"}
```

In this example:

- @pytest.fixture: The client() fixture sets up a test client for the Flask app, allowing us to make HTTP requests during tests.
- client.get('/greet'): This sends a GET request to the /greet endpoint.
- The test checks the **status code** and the **response content** to ensure they match the expected values.

Running Tests with Pytest

Once the test is written, you can run it with the following command:

CopyEdit

```
pytest
```

Pytest will automatically discover all test files starting with `test_` or ending with `_test.py` and run all the test functions inside them.

Using Flask-Testing for More Complex Flask Tests

Flask-Testing is a Flask extension that provides utilities for testing Flask applications. It simplifies testing by providing features such as:

- **Access to the Flask app and client.**
- **Support for setting up and tearing down test data.**
- **Helpers for working with database models.**

Here's how you can use **Flask-Testing** for more advanced Flask tests:

python
CopyEdit

```python
from flask_testing import TestCase
from app import app

class TestGreetEndpoint(TestCase):
    def create_app(self):
        app.config['TESTING'] = True  # Enable testing mode
        return app

    def test_greet(self):
        response = self.client.get('/greet')
        self.assertEqual(response.status_code, 200)
        self.assertEqual(response.json, {"message": "Hello, World!"})
```

In this example:

- `create_app()` is a required method when using Flask-Testing. It allows you to configure your Flask app for testing.
- `self.client.get('/greet')` makes a request to the /greet endpoint.

114

- self.assertEqual() is used to assert that the response status code and content are correct.

Flask-Testing provides extra functionality over Pytest, particularly for managing application contexts and integrating with the Flask app's lifecycle.

7.3 Writing Test Cases for Flask API Endpoints

Writing test cases for Flask API endpoints is crucial to ensure the functionality and reliability of your application. A good test case should verify that an endpoint behaves as expected for a variety of inputs, including edge cases.

1. Testing GET Requests

GET requests are typically used to retrieve data from the server. When testing GET endpoints, you should verify that the correct data is returned, and the correct HTTP status code is sent.

Example: Testing a list of users:

```python
CopyEdit
def test_get_users(client):
    response = client.get('/users')
    assert response.status_code == 200
    assert len(response.json) > 0  # Ensure there is at least one user
```

In this example:

- The test checks that the response status code is 200 OK.
- It also checks that the response body contains a list of users.

2. Testing POST Requests

POST requests are used to create new resources. When testing POST endpoints, you should validate that the new resource is created correctly and that the correct HTTP status code is returned.

115

Example: Testing user creation:

python
CopyEdit
```
def test_create_user(client):
    new_user = {"username": "john_doe", "email": "john@example.com"}
    response = client.post('/users', json=new_user)
    assert response.status_code == 201
    assert response.json['username'] == 'john_doe'
    assert response.json['email'] == 'john@example.com'
```

In this example:

- The test sends a POST request with a new user's data.
- It verifies that the server returns a 201 Created status code and that the response contains the correct user data.

3. Testing PUT Requests

PUT requests are used to update an existing resource. When testing PUT endpoints, ensure that the resource is updated correctly.

Example: Testing user update:

python
CopyEdit
```
def test_update_user(client):
    user_update = {"email": "newemail@example.com"}
    response = client.put('/users/1', json=user_update)
    assert response.status_code == 200
    assert response.json['email'] == 'newemail@example.com'
```

In this example:

- The test sends a PUT request to update the email of the user with ID 1.
- It checks that the email was correctly updated and the status code is 200 OK.

4. Testing DELETE Requests

DELETE requests are used to remove a resource. When testing DELETE endpoints, ensure that the resource is deleted and that the correct status code is returned.

116

Example: Testing user deletion:

python
CopyEdit

```
def test_delete_user(client):
    response = client.delete('/users/1')
    assert response.status_code == 204
    # Ensure that the user no longer exists
    response = client.get('/users/1')
    assert response.status_code == 404
```

In this example:

- The test sends a DELETE request to remove the user with ID 1.
- It verifies that the status code is 204 No Content and checks that the user is no longer accessible by sending a GET request.

5. Testing Error Handling

API error handling is crucial for providing meaningful responses when something goes wrong. Ensure that your API returns appropriate error messages and status codes for invalid input or missing resources.

Example: Testing invalid input:

python
CopyEdit

```
def test_invalid_user_creation(client):
    invalid_user = {"username": "", "email": "invalidemail"}
    response = client.post('/users', json=invalid_user)
    assert response.status_code == 400  # Bad Request
    assert 'error' in response.json
```

In this example:

- The test sends invalid data (empty username and invalid email).
- It checks that the server returns a 400 Bad Request status code and provides an error message.

117

Best Practices for Writing Test Cases

- **Cover Edge Cases**: Make sure your tests cover common and edge cases, such as invalid input, missing data, and incorrect formats.
- **Test Authentication and Authorization**: Test your authentication and authorization logic to ensure that only authorized users can access protected resources.
- **Use Fixtures for Test Data**: Use fixtures to set up test data before each test and clean up afterward to ensure consistency and avoid data contamination between tests.

Testing Flask APIs is crucial for ensuring the stability, security, and correctness of your application. By writing unit tests, integrating Pytest and Flask-Testing, and thoroughly testing all aspects of your API (from basic CRUD operations to error handling and edge cases), you can catch bugs early, avoid regressions, and maintain high-quality code throughout the development lifecycle. With Flask's simple testing utilities and Pytest's powerful features, you can easily test your Flask API endpoints and ensure that your API behaves as expected

7.4 Mocking Requests and Responses

In real-world applications, APIs often interact with external services such as databases, third-party APIs, or payment gateways. During testing, however, it's not always feasible or desirable to make real requests to these services, as doing so might slow down the tests, introduce external dependencies, or even cause unintentional modifications to data. **Mocking** allows you to simulate these interactions without actually calling the external services, enabling faster and more isolated tests.

Mocking is a crucial part of unit testing because it ensures that the tests focus only on the logic of the application rather than its dependencies.

Why Use Mocking in API Testing?

1. **Isolate the Code**: Mocking isolates the code being tested from external systems. This ensures that tests are not dependent on external APIs or databases.
2. **Speed**: Mocked responses are faster than making real requests, which speeds up the testing process.
3. **Reliability**: Tests that depend on external systems might fail due to downtime or changes in those systems. Mocking eliminates this risk.

4. **Control**: Mocking allows you to control the behavior of external services, making it easier to test error handling and edge cases.

Mocking with unittest.mock in Python

Python's built-in unittest.mock module is a powerful tool for mocking in unit tests. It allows you to replace parts of your code with mock objects and assert that specific behaviors occurred.

For example, suppose your Flask application makes a request to an external API to fetch user data:

python

CopyEdit

```python
import requests

from flask import Flask, jsonify

app = Flask(__name__)

@app.route('/get_user_data')

def get_user_data():

    response = requests.get('https://api.example.com/user')

    data = response.json()

    return jsonify(data)
```

You can mock the requests.get() call in your test:

python

CopyEdit

```python
import pytest

from unittest.mock import patch

from app import app
```
119

```python
@pytest.fixture
def client():
    with app.test_client() as client:
        yield client

def test_get_user_data(client):
    # Mock the 'requests.get' method
    with patch('requests.get') as mock_get:
        mock_get.return_value.json.return_value = {'id': 1, 'username': 'john_doe'}

        # Test the endpoint
        response = client.get('/get_user_data')
        assert response.status_code == 200
        assert response.json == {'id': 1, 'username': 'john_doe'}
```

In this example:

- patch('requests.get') replaces the requests.get() call with a mock object.
- mock_get.return_value.json.return_value simulates the response from the external API.
- The test ensures that the Flask application correctly returns the mocked user data without actually making an HTTP request.

Mocking Responses for Flask Routes

When mocking responses, you may want to mock HTTP status codes or simulate specific scenarios, such as failed requests or timeouts. Here's an example of mocking a failed response:

python

CopyEdit

```python
def test_get_user_data_failure(client):
    with patch('requests.get') as mock_get:
        mock_get.return_value.status_code = 500  # Simulate server error
        mock_get.return_value.json.return_value = {'error': 'Server Error'}
        response = client.get('/get_user_data')
        assert response.status_code == 500
        assert response.json == {'error': 'Server Error'}
```

This test simulates a server error (HTTP 500) and verifies that the Flask application correctly handles the error.

Best Practices for Mocking

- **Avoid Mocking Too Much**: Mocking is useful for isolating external dependencies, but avoid mocking too much of the internal application logic. Over-mocking can lead to tests that don't truly reflect how the application will behave in production.
- **Use Fixtures for Reusable Mock Data**: If your tests require a lot of repeated mock data, consider using Pytest fixtures to set up reusable mocks.
- **Mock Responses for Both Success and Failure**: Ensure your tests cover both successful and failing interactions with external services to fully test your error handling.

7.5 Debugging Common Issues in Flask Applications

Even the most well-written Flask applications encounter bugs or issues during development and production. Efficient debugging is crucial to identifying and resolving these issues quickly. Flask provides several built-in tools and practices to help with debugging.

121

Common Flask Debugging Techniques

1. Using app.debug and Flask's Built-in Debugger

Flask has a built-in debugger that helps identify issues by providing detailed error messages and stack traces when an error occurs during development. To enable debugging in Flask, you can set the debug mode to True:

python

CopyEdit

```
app = Flask(__name__)

app.debug = True
```

With debug=True, Flask will automatically show detailed error pages when an exception occurs, including the traceback and local variables. However, it's important to remember that this should **never** be enabled in production environments, as it can expose sensitive information.

2. Using flask run with Debug Mode

Instead of setting app.debug = True manually, you can also run the Flask application with the --debugger flag using the flask run command:

bash

CopyEdit

```
flask run --debugger
```

This starts the application with the debugger enabled, and it will catch exceptions and provide detailed output in the terminal.

3. Viewing Stack Traces

Flask automatically provides detailed stack traces in the development environment. This helps pinpoint the exact location where an error occurred in the code. The stack trace shows the sequence of function calls leading up to the error, along with the specific line number that caused it.

122

4. **Logging Errors**

In addition to using Flask's built-in debugger, you can log errors to get better visibility into the issues. Flask integrates well with Python's standard logging library, allowing you to log both errors and general application activities.

python

CopyEdit

```python
import logging

app = Flask(__name__)

# Set up logging

app.logger.setLevel(logging.ERROR)

@app.route('/error')

def error_route():

    try:

        # Simulate an error

        raise ValueError("An example error")

    except Exception as e:

        app.logger.error(f"Error occurred: {str(e)}")

        return "An error occurred", 500
```

In this example:

- The app.logger object is used to log errors at the ERROR level.
- When an exception is caught, it is logged, and a user-friendly error message is returned.

5. **Breakpoints and Debugging in IDEs**

Flask integrates well with popular integrated development environments (IDEs) like **PyCharm**, **VS Code**, and **Eclipse**. These IDEs allow you to set **breakpoints** and use interactive debuggers to pause the application at a specific line of code, inspect variables, and step through the code line by line.

6. **Testing Endpoints and Responses**

When debugging API-specific issues, you can use tools like **Postman** or **cURL** to manually test Flask routes. This allows you to simulate various HTTP requests and inspect the responses directly, which can help identify issues with routing, request handling, and response formatting.

7.6 Using Flask-DebugToolbar for Development

Flask-DebugToolbar is a Flask extension that provides a powerful debugging tool to inspect various aspects of your application while it's running. It adds a debugging toolbar to the top of your web pages during development, allowing you to interactively inspect and diagnose issues without interrupting the application flow.

Installing Flask-DebugToolbar

To get started, install Flask-DebugToolbar via pip:

bash

CopyEdit

```
pip install flask-debugtoolbar
```

Setting Up Flask-DebugToolbar

To use Flask-DebugToolbar in your Flask app, import the extension and configure it as follows:

python

CopyEdit

```
from flask import Flask
```

```python
from flask_debugtoolbar import DebugToolbarExtension

app = Flask(__name__)

app.config['DEBUG_TB_INTERCEPT_REDIRECTS'] = False  # Disable redirects being intercepted

app.config['SECRET_KEY'] = 'your_secret_key'


toolbar = DebugToolbarExtension(app)


@app.route('/')

def home():

    return 'Hello, Flask Debug Toolbar!'


if __name__ == '__main__':

    app.run(debug=True)
```

In this example:

- DEBUG_TB_INTERCEPT_REDIRECTS is set to False to prevent Flask-DebugToolbar from intercepting redirects and causing issues with the application flow.
- SECRET_KEY is required for Flask-DebugToolbar to function properly, as it relies on secure cookies for its session data.

Features of Flask-DebugToolbar

1. **Request Information**: Flask-DebugToolbar shows detailed information about incoming requests, including the request URL, method, headers, cookies, and form data.
2. **SQL Queries**: If your application interacts with a database, the toolbar provides an interactive view of all SQL queries executed during the request, allowing you to track database interactions and optimize queries.
3. **Template Rendering**: It provides insights into the templates rendered during the request, including the template used, variables passed, and rendering time.
4. **Application Context**: Flask-DebugToolbar displays information about the Flask application context, including request and session data, enabling you to track state changes and debug session-related issues.
5. **Performance Profiling**: It allows you to profile the performance of your application by displaying the time taken by each route and database query.
6. **Error Traceback**: If an error occurs, Flask-DebugToolbar provides a detailed traceback with clickable links that navigate to the exact line of code where the error occurred.

Flask-DebugToolbar is an essential tool for developers working on Flask APIs. It provides real-time insight into various aspects of your application, helping you diagnose issues quickly and efficiently. By combining Flask-DebugToolbar with Python's built-in debugging tools, logging, and manual testing, you can ensure that your application runs smoothly during development and is easier to maintain in production

Chapter 8: Optimizing Flask APIs for Performance

8.1 Improving Response Times and Latency

The performance of your API is crucial to providing a seamless experience for users and ensuring that your application can scale to handle increasing traffic. **Response time** and **latency** are two key metrics for API performance. Response time is the amount of time it takes for your API to process a request and return a response, while latency refers to the delay in transferring data between the client and the server.

When building a Flask API, there are several strategies you can use to reduce response times and improve the overall performance of your application. Below are key techniques for enhancing API response times:

1. Minimize Server-Side Processing

A common cause of slow response times is the time taken to process a request on the server side. You can reduce the server-side processing time by:

- **Optimizing Business Logic**: Make sure your code is efficient, eliminating unnecessary operations or redundant calculations. For example, avoid complex calculations or data processing inside view functions if they can be handled in background tasks.
- **Asynchronous Processing**: For operations that are time-consuming (like sending emails or interacting with third-party services), consider processing them asynchronously using background jobs. **Celery** is a popular library for asynchronous task queues in Python.
- **Defer Non-Critical Operations**: Defer non-critical tasks that do not need to be part of the API response (like logging or email sending) by handling them after the response is sent back to the client.

2. Reduce Payload Size

Large response payloads increase the time it takes to serialize and transmit data. Consider the following strategies to reduce payload size:

- **Use Efficient Data Formats**: When sending large amounts of data, consider using efficient serialization formats like **JSON** or **Protocol Buffers**. Avoid XML or other verbose formats that require more bandwidth.

Return Only Necessary Data: Ensure that your API returns only the data that is required by the client. Avoid sending unnecessary fields that the client doesn't need. This is especially important when dealing with large datasets.
For example, instead of returning all fields of a user record, you could return only the fields that are relevant to the specific request:
python
CopyEdit
```
@app.route('/user/<int:user_id>')
def get_user(user_id):
    user = User.query.filter_by(id=user_id).first()
    return jsonify({
        "username": user.username,
        "email": user.email  # Only return necessary fields
    })
```

3. Optimize API Endpoints and Routes

API route structure and endpoint design can impact response times. Here are some practices to improve performance:

- **Avoid Complex and Deeply Nested Routes**: Keep route URLs simple and avoid excessive nesting, which can lead to performance issues due to the complexity of routing and database queries.

Route Filtering: Ensure that your routes handle filters or query parameters efficiently. For example, when returning a list of records from the database, apply filters to minimize the number of records returned. Only return records that match the client's query.

For example:
python
CopyEdit

```python
@app.route('/users')
def get_users():
    query = User.query
    username = request.args.get('username')
    if username:
        query = query.filter_by(username=username)
    users = query.all()
    return jsonify([user.username for user in users])
```

4. Use Connection Pools for Database Access

Database connections can be slow, and opening and closing a connection for each request can add significant latency. Using a **connection pool** to manage and reuse database connections can greatly reduce the time spent on database interactions. Flask extensions like **SQLAlchemy** come with connection pooling support out of the box, but you can also configure the pool size and timeout to better suit your application's needs.

Example with **SQLAlchemy**:

python
CopyEdit

```python
app.config['SQLALCHEMY_POOL_SIZE'] = 10
app.config['SQLALCHEMY_POOL_TIMEOUT'] = 30
```

5. Content Compression

Another way to improve response times is by reducing the size of the data transmitted between the server and the client. **HTTP compression** (using algorithms like **gzip** or **deflate**) reduces the size of the response payload, making it faster for the client to download the data.

To enable **gzip compression** in Flask, you can use the Flask-Compress extension:

bash
CopyEdit
```
pip install Flask-Compress
```

python
CopyEdit
```
from flask import Flask
from flask_compress import Compress

app = Flask(__name__)
Compress(app)

@app.route('/data')
def get_data():
    return jsonify({"data": "This is a large dataset that will be compressed"})
```

This reduces the size of responses, improving response times, particularly for users with slower connections.

6. Rate Limiting

Rate limiting helps prevent abuse of your API by controlling the number of requests that a client can make in a given time frame. This is crucial for preventing denial-of-service (DoS) attacks and ensuring fair usage of server resources. Flask extensions like **Flask-Limiter** provide an easy way to implement rate limiting.

bash
CopyEdit
```
pip install Flask-Limiter
```

python
CopyEdit
```
from flask import Flask
from flask_limiter import Limiter

app = Flask(__name__)
```

130

```
limiter = Limiter(app, key_func=get_remote_address)

@app.route('/api')
@limiter.limit("5 per minute")
def limited_api():
    return "This API is rate-limited"
```

This example limits the number of requests to 5 per minute for the /api route.

8.2 Caching with Flask-Caching

Caching is a technique used to store frequently accessed data temporarily in memory to speed up subsequent access. By caching responses, you can drastically reduce the time spent on generating the same data over and over, reducing both response times and server load.

Why Use Caching in Flask?

1. **Improve Response Time**: Cached data can be served almost instantaneously, leading to faster response times.
2. **Reduce Load on Database**: Caching helps reduce the load on your database by avoiding repeated database queries for the same data.
3. **Lower Latency**: With cached data, your API can serve data much faster, especially when handling frequently requested resources.
4. **Save Resources**: By serving cached responses, you save processing power and bandwidth, reducing operational costs.

Setting Up Flask-Caching

To use caching in Flask, you can use the **Flask-Caching** extension. First, install it:

bash
CopyEdit
```
pip install Flask-Caching
```

Then, configure Flask-Caching in your Flask app:

python
CopyEdit
```
from flask import Flask
from flask_caching import Cache

app = Flask(__name__)
cache = Cache(app, config={'CACHE_TYPE': 'simple'})  # Simple in-memory cache

@app.route('/data')
@cache.cached(timeout=60)  # Cache this endpoint for 60 seconds
def get_data():
    # Simulate an expensive operation
    return {'data': 'This data is cached for 60 seconds'}
```

In this example:

- The @cache.cached() decorator is used to cache the response of the get_data() function for 60 seconds.
- The next time the same request is made within 60 seconds, the cached response is returned, reducing processing time.

Cache Types

Flask-Caching supports several caching backends:

- **Simple Cache**: Stores data in memory (default for testing purposes).
- **Memcached**: A distributed memory caching system that stores data in RAM, often used in production environments.
- **Redis**: A more robust and scalable caching solution than Memcached. Redis stores data in-memory but also persists it on disk.

You can configure your cache backend like this:

python
CopyEdit
```
app.config['CACHE_TYPE'] = 'redis'
app.config['CACHE_REDIS_URL'] = "redis://localhost:6379/0"
```

```
cache = Cache(app)
```

Cache Invalidation

Cache invalidation is the process of removing stale or outdated data from the cache. You need to implement cache invalidation logic whenever your data changes. For example, if a user updates their profile information, you may want to clear the cache for that user's profile.

You can manually invalidate the cache using:

python
CopyEdit
```
cache.delete('profile_user_123')
```

In this example, the cache for the user profile with ID 123 is cleared.

8.3 Optimizing Database Queries

The database is often the bottleneck in API performance. **Slow queries** can significantly degrade response times, especially when handling large amounts of data. Optimizing database queries is essential to improving the performance of your Flask API.

1. Use Indexes for Faster Queries

Indexes are data structures that allow the database to find rows faster than by scanning the entire table. When querying a database for specific fields, ensure that indexes are created on those fields. This is especially important for fields that are used frequently in WHERE clauses or as part of JOIN operations.

For example, in SQLAlchemy (Flask's default ORM), you can add indexes like this:

python
CopyEdit
```
class User(db.Model):
    id = db.Column(db.Integer, primary_key=True)
    username = db.Column(db.String(80), unique=True, nullable=False, index=True)
    email = db.Column(db.String(120), unique=True, nullable=False)
```

133

In this example, the username column has an index to speed up queries that filter by username.

2. Use Query Optimization Techniques

Flask, along with **SQLAlchemy**, provides various methods for optimizing queries. Here are some tips for writing efficient database queries:

Avoid N+1 Query Problems: When querying related models, use joinedload or subqueryload to eager load relationships. This prevents SQLAlchemy from issuing additional queries for each related object.
Example:
python
CopyEdit

```
from sqlalchemy.orm import joinedload

users = User.query.options(joinedload(User.posts)).all()
```

Limit the Number of Retrieved Records: If you only need a subset of records, make sure to limit the number of records returned with .limit() or .slice(). Always avoid retrieving more data than necessary.
Example:
python
CopyEdit

```
users = User.query.limit(10).all()
```

- **Use .filter() Efficiently**: When applying filters to your queries, try to make use of indexes and avoid using LIKE or OR clauses, as these can be slower.

Use .paginate() for Large Results: Instead of returning all records at once, paginate large datasets to return only a small number of records at a time.
Example:
python
CopyEdit

```
users = User.query.paginate(page=1, per_page=10, error_out=False)
```

3. Optimize Joins and Subqueries

When performing **joins** or **subqueries**, ensure that you are not retrieving unnecessary data. If a subquery or join is expensive, try to limit it or optimize it by adding proper indexes and only retrieving the columns that are necessary for the current operation.

For example, using exists() or in_() for subqueries can be more efficient than retrieving all rows:

python
CopyEdit
```
from sqlalchemy.orm import aliased

user_subquery = User.query.filter(User.email == 'example@example.com').exists()
posts = Post.query.filter(user_subquery).all()
```

4. Use Query Caching

You can use caching at the database query level. By caching frequently used database queries, you can reduce the number of calls to the database. This is particularly useful for read-heavy APIs.

Example:

python
CopyEdit
```
@app.route('/users')
@cache.cached(timeout=60)
def get_users():
    users = User.query.all()
    return jsonify([user.username for user in users])
```

In this example, the result of the User.query.all() query is cached for 60 seconds, avoiding multiple database calls for the same request.

Optimizing database queries and using caching strategies can greatly enhance the performance of your Flask API. Indexing key columns, optimizing queries, and implementing caching mechanisms ensure that your application performs well under load and remains scalable as it grows. By applying these best practices, you can significantly improve response times, reduce latency, and enhance the overall performance of your Flask application.

8.4 Managing Long-Running Tasks with Celery

Handling long-running tasks in a web application can significantly impact performance, especially when those tasks need to be processed asynchronously. Examples of long-running tasks include sending emails, processing images or videos, or interacting with third-party services. If these tasks are executed synchronously within an API request, they can block the server, resulting in slow response times and poor user experience.

Celery is a powerful distributed task queue that allows you to manage background tasks asynchronously. It enables you to offload tasks to worker processes, freeing up the main application thread to handle new incoming requests.

Why Use Celery?

1. **Asynchronous Task Processing**: Celery allows you to handle tasks asynchronously, meaning tasks that would otherwise block the main thread are executed in the background.
2. **Scalability**: Celery supports scaling by running multiple worker processes, which enables you to handle a large number of tasks simultaneously.
3. **Retry Logic**: Celery provides built-in retry mechanisms for failed tasks, helping ensure reliability even if a task fails temporarily.
4. **Task Scheduling**: Celery integrates with **Celery Beat**, a scheduler that allows you to run periodic tasks (such as cleaning up the database or sending reminder emails).

Setting Up Celery with Flask

1. **Install Celery and Redis**

Celery requires a message broker to handle task queues. **Redis** is a popular message broker for Celery because it is fast and easy to set up.

Install the necessary packages:

bash

CopyEdit

```
pip install celery redis
```

2. **Create a Celery Instance**

In your Flask application, create a Celery instance that connects to Redis as the message broker:

python

CopyEdit

```
from flask import Flask
from celery import Celery


app = Flask(__name__)


# Configure Celery to use Redis as the message broker
app.config['CELERY_BROKER_URL'] = 'redis://localhost:6379/0'
app.config['CELERY_RESULT_BACKEND'] = 'redis://localhost:6379/0'
```

137

```python
# Create Celery instance
celery = Celery(app.name, broker=app.config['CELERY_BROKER_URL'])
celery.conf.update(app.config)
```

3. **Define a Long-Running Task**

Now, define a task that will be processed in the background:

python

CopyEdit

```python
@celery.task(bind=True)
def long_running_task(self):
    try:
        # Simulate a long-running task (e.g., sending emails)
        time.sleep(10)  # Example of long-running task
        return 'Task Completed'
    except Exception as e:
        raise self.retry(exc=e)
```

In this example:

- The @celery.task decorator defines a Celery task.
- The time.sleep(10) simulates a long-running task that would otherwise block the server.
- The self.retry() method allows automatic retries in case of failure.
4. **Trigger the Task from an Endpoint**

138

To trigger the task from a Flask route, you can call the delay() method on the task:

python

CopyEdit

```
@app.route('/start_task', methods=['GET'])

def start_task():

    long_running_task.apply_async()  # Trigger the background task asynchronously

    return "Task started in the background!", 202
```

When a request is made to /start_task, the task is executed in the background, and the server can immediately respond to the client without waiting for the task to complete.

Handling Task Results

You can retrieve the results of a task after it has been processed:

python

CopyEdit

```
@app.route('/get_task_result/<task_id>', methods=['GET'])

def get_task_result(task_id):

    task = long_running_task.AsyncResult(task_id)

    if task.state == 'SUCCESS':

        return jsonify({'status': 'Task completed', 'result': task.result})

    elif task.state == 'PENDING':

        return jsonify({'status': 'Task is still pending'})

    else:
```

```
return jsonify({'status': 'Task failed', 'result': task.info})
```

This endpoint allows you to check the status of the task by its task_id.

Running Celery Workers

To process tasks asynchronously, you must run Celery workers separately from the Flask application. Start the worker from the command line:

bash

CopyEdit

```
celery -A app.celery worker
```

This command will start Celery workers that listen for new tasks and process them in the background.

8.5 Profiling Flask Applications for Performance

To improve the performance of your Flask application, you need to understand where the bottlenecks lie. Profiling allows you to measure various performance metrics, identify areas that need optimization, and make data-driven decisions about how to improve your API's speed and scalability.

Why Profiling Matters

Profiling is the process of measuring the performance of your application by analyzing things like response times, memory usage, and CPU usage. Profiling helps you:

1. **Identify Bottlenecks**: Pinpoint which parts of your code are slow or inefficient.
2. **Optimize Code**: Focus your optimization efforts on the areas that matter the most.
3. **Understand Resource Usage**: See how much CPU and memory your application is consuming, which helps in scaling and improving resource efficiency.

Flask Profiling Tools

    1. **Flask-Profiler**

Flask-Profiler is an extension that provides basic performance profiling by tracking the time spent on each request and route.

To install Flask-Profiler:

bash

CopyEdit

```
pip install flask-profiler
```

Next, set up Flask-Profiler in your Flask application:

python

CopyEdit

```
from flask import Flask
from flask_profiler import Profiler
app = Flask(__name__)


# Configure Flask-Profiler
app.config["FLASK_PROFILER"] = {
    "enabled": True,
    "storage": {
        "engine": "sqlite",
        "file_name": "profiler.db"
    }
```

```
:
profiler = Profiler(app)


@app.route('/')
def home():
    return "Flask Profiler Example"


if __name__ == '__main__':
    app.run(debug=True)
```

Once enabled, Flask-Profiler automatically logs the execution times of all requests, which can then be viewed through an interactive web interface.

2. cProfile

cProfile is a built-in Python module that can be used to profile the performance of your Flask application. It provides a detailed breakdown of where time is spent in your code.

To use cProfile:

python

CopyEdit

```
import cProfile
from flask import Flask


app = Flask(__name__)
```

```python
@app.route('/')

def home():

    return "Flask cProfile Example"


if __name__ == '__main__':

    cProfile.run('app.run(debug=True)')
```

cProfile will generate a performance report, detailing the time spent in each function and method. This can help you identify slow parts of your code that need optimization.

3. **Werkzeug Profiler**

Flask uses **Werkzeug** as its WSGI server, and Werkzeug has a built-in profiler. By enabling the profiler, you can track the performance of each request and view detailed information about the execution time and functions involved.

You can enable the profiler in development mode:

python

CopyEdit

```python
from flask import Flask

import werkzeug

app = Flask(__name__)


@app.route('/')

def home():

    return "Werkzeug Profiler Example"
```

```
if __name__ == '__main__':

    app.debug = True

    werkzeug.serving.run_simple('localhost', 5000, app, use_debugger=True,
use_reloader=True)
```

When use_debugger=True is set, Werkzeug will show detailed performance logs, including the request and response processing times.

Key Metrics to Profile

1. **Request Handling Time**: The time it takes to handle incoming requests, including routing, view function execution, and response preparation.
2. **Database Queries**: The time spent in database queries, including the number of queries executed.
3. **Template Rendering**: The time spent rendering HTML templates (if applicable).
4. **External API Calls**: The time taken for API requests to third-party services.

8.6 Load Testing and Stress Testing Your APIs

Testing the performance of your API under load is critical to ensure that it can handle the demands of real-world usage. **Load testing** and **stress testing** are two types of performance testing that simulate different conditions to identify how your API behaves under varying levels of traffic.

1. What is Load Testing?

Load testing involves simulating a normal or expected amount of traffic to understand how your API performs under regular usage. This helps identify performance issues like slow response times or server crashes when handling a large number of requests.

2. What is Stress Testing?

Stress testing goes beyond load testing by pushing the system to its limits. It simulates traffic that exceeds the normal expected levels, helping you determine how the API behaves when overwhelmed by excessive load. Stress testing helps identify critical failure points, such as server crashes or resource exhaustion, and ensures your API is resilient under extreme conditions.

3. Tools for Load Testing and Stress Testing

Several tools can help you simulate traffic and analyze the performance of your Flask API under load. Some of the most popular options include:

1. **Apache JMeter**

Apache JMeter is an open-source tool designed for load testing and performance measurement. It can simulate multiple users, send requests to your API, and collect data on response times, throughput, and error rates.

To use JMeter:

- Download and install JMeter from the official site.
- Create a test plan that simulates users sending requests to your Flask API.
- Analyze the results to identify bottlenecks in your API.
2. **Locust**

Locust is another popular tool for load testing Flask APIs. It allows you to write test scenarios in Python and simulate traffic at different scales.

To install Locust:

bash

CopyEdit

```
pip install locust
```

Example test with Locust:

python

CopyEdit

```
from locust import HttpUser, task, between

class APIUser(HttpUser):
    wait_time = between(1, 2)  # Simulate wait time between requests
```

```
@task
def get_home(self):
    self.client.get("/")
```

You can run Locust with the following command:

bash

CopyEdit

```
locust -f locustfile.py
```

Locust will start a web interface that you can use to configure the load test and analyze the results.

3. **Gatling**

Gatling is another powerful open-source tool for performance testing. It allows you to simulate complex scenarios and run load and stress tests on your API.

4. **Artillery**

Artillery is a modern, lightweight tool for load testing and performance testing APIs. It can simulate thousands of virtual users and provide detailed reports on response times, throughput, and other metrics.

To install Artillery:

bash

CopyEdit

```
npm install -g artillery
```

146

Example command to start load testing:

bash

CopyEdit

artillery quick --duration 30s -c 10 http://localhost:5000/

This command runs a 30-second test with 10 virtual users.

Best Practices for Load and Stress Testing

- **Test with Realistic Traffic**: Simulate real user behavior and traffic patterns to understand how your API will perform under typical usage conditions.
- **Gradually Increase Load**: Start with a small number of users and gradually increase the load to identify how the system behaves as traffic grows.
- **Monitor Server Resources**: During load and stress tests, monitor server metrics like CPU usage, memory usage, and network bandwidth to identify resource bottlenecks.
- **Identify Failure Points**: Stress testing is particularly useful for identifying where your API will fail when the load exceeds its capacity. Use this information to improve system resilience.

Load and stress testing are critical to ensuring that your Flask API can handle both expected and extreme levels of traffic. By using tools like JMeter, Locust, and Artillery, you can simulate traffic, analyze your API's performance, and identify areas that need optimization. Stress testing helps you ensure your API can handle the worst-case scenarios, while load testing ensures smooth performance during normal usage.

Chapter 9: Advanced Flask Techniques

9.1 Introduction to Flask Extensions

Flask is a lightweight and flexible micro-framework for Python that provides the basic tools for building web applications. However, as your application grows in complexity, you may need additional functionality such as database integration, user authentication, or API development. This is where **Flask extensions** come into play.

Flask extensions are add-ons that provide extra features to your Flask application, enabling you to implement common functionality without having to manually write all the code. These extensions integrate seamlessly into your Flask application, following its minimalistic philosophy while providing powerful, modular components.

Why Use Flask Extensions?

1. **Faster Development**: Extensions provide pre-built, reusable components, enabling you to implement common features quickly and efficiently without reinventing the wheel.
2. **Modularity**: Flask's lightweight core is extended through these modular components, allowing you to add only the functionality you need without bloating your application.
3. **Scalability**: Many Flask extensions are designed to work well for both small projects and large, production-level applications, making them a perfect fit as your app grows.
4. **Community Support**: Flask's extensions are often developed and maintained by the Flask community or other Python developers, ensuring that the code is well-tested and widely used in production environments.

Popular Flask Extensions

Some of the most commonly used Flask extensions include:

- **Flask-SQLAlchemy**: An ORM (Object Relational Mapping) extension that simplifies working with relational databases like PostgreSQL and MySQL.
- **Flask-WTF**: Provides integration with WTForms to simplify handling forms and validation in Flask applications.
- **Flask-Login**: An extension for managing user sessions and authentication, enabling login and logout functionality.

- **Flask-Mail**: Simplifies sending email from Flask applications.
- **Flask-RESTful**: A powerful extension for building REST APIs in Flask by providing tools for defining resources and handling HTTP methods.

How Flask Extensions Work

Flask extensions generally integrate with Flask via the application instance, providing additional functionality to the app. Extensions typically do not modify Flask's core behavior but instead introduce specific features that can be initialized and configured at runtime.

For example, to use **Flask-SQLAlchemy** in your Flask application, you would install the extension and then initialize it with your app:

bash
CopyEdit
```
pip install flask-sqlalchemy
```

python
CopyEdit
```
from flask import Flask
from flask_sqlalchemy import SQLAlchemy

app = Flask(__name__)
app.config['SQLALCHEMY_DATABASE_URI'] = 'sqlite:///example.db'

db = SQLAlchemy(app)
```

In this example, we have initialized **SQLAlchemy** as an extension and configured it with the database URI for our Flask app.

Best Practices for Using Flask Extensions

- **Choose Extensions Carefully**: Flask has a rich ecosystem of extensions. Choose the ones that best fit your application's needs and check their documentation for compatibility and limitations.
- **Keep It Lightweight**: Only include the extensions you truly need. Flask's philosophy is minimalism, so avoid adding unnecessary overhead by using too many extensions.

- **Read the Documentation**: While extensions are often easy to integrate, each one has its own configuration and setup guidelines. Always read the documentation for the extension you're using to ensure you're implementing it correctly.

9.2 Using Flask-SQLAlchemy for Database Integration

Flask-SQLAlchemy is one of the most popular Flask extensions, providing an easy and efficient way to interact with databases using **SQLAlchemy**, which is a powerful Object Relational Mapper (ORM). It allows you to define and query database models using Python classes, abstracting away raw SQL and making it easier to work with relational databases.

Why Use Flask-SQLAlchemy?

1. **Object Relational Mapping (ORM)**: Flask-SQLAlchemy simplifies database interactions by allowing you to work with Python objects instead of raw SQL queries. This leads to more readable and maintainable code.
2. **Database Abstraction**: With Flask-SQLAlchemy, you don't need to worry about the specifics of the database engine, as it abstracts away the underlying database interactions.
3. **Supports Multiple Databases**: Flask-SQLAlchemy supports multiple relational databases, including PostgreSQL, MySQL, and SQLite, and allows you to switch between them with minimal code changes.

Setting Up Flask-SQLAlchemy

To use **Flask-SQLAlchemy**, first install it using pip:

```bash
CopyEdit
pip install flask-sqlalchemy
```

Next, configure it in your Flask application:

python
CopyEdit

```python
from flask import Flask
from flask_sqlalchemy import SQLAlchemy

app = Flask(__name__)
app.config['SQLALCHEMY_DATABASE_URI'] = 'sqlite:///example.db'
app.config['SQLALCHEMY_TRACK_MODIFICATIONS'] = False  # Disable
modification tracking

db = SQLAlchemy(app)
```

In this example:

- We configure **SQLAlchemy** to use an SQLite database (example.db).
- The SQLALCHEMY_TRACK_MODIFICATIONS configuration is set to False
  to disable Flask-SQLAlchemy's tracking of modifications, which can reduce
  overhead.

Defining Models

Flask-SQLAlchemy uses Python classes to define database models. Each model
represents a table in the database, and each class attribute represents a column in the
table. You can also define relationships between tables using SQLAlchemy's features.

python
CopyEdit

```python
class User(db.Model):
    id = db.Column(db.Integer, primary_key=True)
    username = db.Column(db.String(100), unique=True, nullable=False)
    email = db.Column(db.String(120), unique=True, nullable=False)

    def __repr__(self):
        return f'<User {self.username}>'
```

In this example:

- The User class represents a table in the database with three columns: id, username, and email.
- The id column is the primary key and automatically generates unique values for each row.
- The __repr__() method provides a string representation of the model, which is useful for debugging.

Interacting with the Database

Once your models are defined, you can interact with the database by querying, inserting, updating, or deleting records using SQLAlchemy's ORM methods.

Creating a New User:

```python
CopyEdit
new_user = User(username='johndoe', email='johndoe@example.com')
db.session.add(new_user)
db.session.commit()
```

Querying Users:

```python
CopyEdit
user = User.query.filter_by(username='johndoe').first()
print(user.email)  # Output: johndoe@example.com
```

Updating a User:

```python
CopyEdit
user = User.query.get(1)  # Get user with ID 1
user.email = 'newemail@example.com'
db.session.commit()
```

Deleting a User:

python
CopyEdit
```
user = User.query.get(1)  # Get user with ID 1
db.session.delete(user)
db.session.commit()
```

Database Migrations with Flask-Migrate

As your application evolves, you'll likely need to make changes to your database schema, such as adding or removing columns. **Flask-Migrate** is an extension that integrates **Alembic**, a database migration tool, with Flask-SQLAlchemy, allowing you to manage database schema changes over time.

To use Flask-Migrate, install it first:

bash
CopyEdit
```
pip install Flask-Migrate
```

Then, initialize Flask-Migrate in your app:

python
CopyEdit
```
from flask_migrate import Migrate

migrate = Migrate(app, db)
```

You can now use the following commands to manage migrations:

- flask db init to initialize migration scripts.
- flask db migrate to generate migration scripts.
- flask db upgrade to apply the migrations to the database.

153

9.3 Flask-RESTful for Building RESTful APIs

Flask-RESTful is an extension for Flask that adds support for quickly building REST APIs. REST (Representational State Transfer) is an architectural style for designing networked applications, and Flask-RESTful simplifies the process of creating RESTful services by providing tools to define resources, handle HTTP methods (GET, POST, PUT, DELETE), and format responses.

Why Use Flask-RESTful?

1. **Simplified API Development**: Flask-RESTful abstracts the complexity of building REST APIs, allowing you to focus on defining resources and handling HTTP requests.
2. **Easy Integration**: Flask-RESTful integrates seamlessly with Flask and doesn't require significant changes to your existing Flask application structure.
3. **Support for Request Parsing**: Flask-RESTful provides easy-to-use request parsers for handling query parameters, JSON payloads, and form data, simplifying the handling of incoming requests.
4. **Built-in Response Formatting**: Flask-RESTful automatically formats the response in JSON, making it easy to serve data to clients in a standardized format.

Setting Up Flask-RESTful

To install Flask-RESTful, use pip:

bash
CopyEdit
```
pip install flask-restful
```

Then, set it up in your Flask app:

python
CopyEdit
```
from flask import Flask
from flask_restful import Api, Resource

app = Flask(__name__)
api = Api(app)
```

154

```
class HelloWorld(Resource):
    def get(self):
        return {'message': 'Hello, World!'}

api.add_resource(HelloWorld, '/')

if __name__ == '__main__':
    app.run(debug=True)
```

In this example:

- We create a new resource class HelloWorld, which inherits from Resource.
- The get() method defines the behavior for GET requests to the / endpoint.
- api.add_resource() adds the HelloWorld resource to the Flask application at the / endpoint.

Handling Different HTTP Methods

Flask-RESTful allows you to define methods for different HTTP verbs (GET, POST, PUT, DELETE) inside the same resource class. Each method corresponds to the respective HTTP request type.

Example with **GET**, **POST**, and **PUT**:

python
CopyEdit
```
class User(Resource):
    def get(self, user_id):
        user = UserModel.query.get(user_id)
        return {'id': user.id, 'username': user.username}, 200
    def post(self):
        data = request.get_json()
        new_user = UserModel(username=data['username'])
        db.session.add(new_user)
        db.session.commit()
        return {'message': 'User created', 'id': new_user.id}, 201
```

```
def put(self, user_id):
    data = request.get_json()
    user = UserModel.query.get(user_id)
    user.username = data['username']
    db.session.commit()
    return {'message': 'User updated'}, 200
```

- **GET** retrieves a user by ID.
- **POST** creates a new user.
- **PUT** updates the username of an existing user.

Parsing Incoming Data

Flask-RESTful provides the reqparse class for parsing incoming data (e.g., JSON, form data, or query parameters). Here's how you can use it to handle POST data:

python
CopyEdit
```
from flask_restful import reqparse

class User(Resource):
    def post(self):
        parser = reqparse.RequestParser()
        parser.add_argument('username', required=True, help="Username cannot be blank")
        args = parser.parse_args()

        new_user = UserModel(username=args['username'])
        db.session.add(new_user)
        db.session.commit()
        return {'message': 'User created', 'id': new_user.id}, 201
```

In this example:

- We use reqparse to validate and parse the incoming JSON data.
- If the username field is missing, Flask-RESTful automatically returns a 400 error with a message indicating that the field is required.

Handling Nested Resources
156

Flask-RESTful allows you to define nested resources, which is useful when dealing with related models (such as users and their posts).

python
CopyEdit
```python
class Post(Resource):
    def get(self, post_id):
        post = PostModel.query.get(post_id)
        return {'id': post.id, 'title': post.title}, 200


class User(Resource):
    def get(self, user_id):
        user = UserModel.query.get(user_id)
        return {'id': user.id, 'username': user.username}, 200

    def add_post(self, user_id):
        user = UserModel.query.get(user_id)
        post = PostModel(title="New Post", user_id=user.id)
        db.session.add(post)
        db.session.commit()
        return {'message': 'Post created', 'id': post.id}, 201
```

Flask-RESTful is a powerful and flexible extension that simplifies the process of building REST APIs with Flask. It provides a clean interface for defining resources and handling HTTP methods, request parsing, and response formatting. By using Flask-RESTful, you can quickly create RESTful services while maintaining the flexibility and simplicity that Flask is known for. Combined with other Flask extensions like Flask-SQLAlchemy, Flask-RESTful is a great choice for building scalable and maintainable APIs.

9.4 WebSockets with Flask for Real-Time Applications

In modern web applications, there is a growing demand for real-time interaction, such as live updates, chat functionality, or notifications. Traditional HTTP requests, where the client makes a request and the server responds, are not well-suited for real-time features because they rely on periodic polling or refreshes to update data. **WebSockets** are a more efficient solution, as they provide a full-duplex communication channel between the client and server over a single, persistent connection.

157

WebSockets allow for real-time, bidirectional communication, meaning the server can push updates to the client without waiting for the client to request them.

Why Use WebSockets with Flask?

1. **Real-Time Interactivity**: WebSockets are ideal for building interactive, real-time features like live chat, notifications, online collaboration, and multiplayer games.
2. **Reduced Latency**: WebSockets eliminate the need for multiple HTTP requests by keeping the connection open, leading to faster communication between the client and the server.
3. **Efficient Data Transfer**: WebSockets use less overhead compared to traditional HTTP polling, making them more efficient when dealing with frequent, small data exchanges.

Setting Up WebSockets with Flask

To implement WebSockets in Flask, you can use **Flask-SocketIO**, which is a Flask extension that enables WebSocket support in Flask applications.

1. **Installing Flask-SocketIO**

To get started, you need to install **Flask-SocketIO**:

bash

CopyEdit

```
pip install flask-socketio
```

2. Creating a Simple Flask WebSocket Server

Now you can create a simple Flask application with WebSocket support using Flask-SocketIO:

python

CopyEdit

```
from flask import Flask, render_template
from flask_socketio import SocketIO, send


app = Flask(__name__)
socketio = SocketIO(app)


@app.route('/')
def index():
    return render_template('index.html')


@socketio.on('message')
def handle_message(message):
    print(f'Received message: {message}')
    send(f'You said: {message}')


if __name__ == '__main__':
    socketio.run(app)
```

In this example:

- We initialize the SocketIO instance with the Flask app.
- The @socketio.on('message') decorator is used to handle incoming WebSocket messages.
- When a message is received, the server responds by sending back the same message with a prefix ("You said: ...").

3. **Client-Side WebSocket Connection**

On the client side, you will need to create an HTML file (e.g., index.html) that connects to the WebSocket server using **Socket.IO**:

html

CopyEdit

```html
<!DOCTYPE html>

<html>

<head>

  <title>WebSocket with Flask</title>

  <script src="https://cdn.socket.io/4.0.0/socket.io.min.js"></script>

  <script type="text/javascript">

    var socket = io.connect('http://' + document.domain + ':' + location.port);


    socket.on('connect', function() {

      console.log('Connected to WebSocket server');

    });
```

```
socket.on('message', function(msg) {

    document.getElementById('messages').innerHTML += '<p>' + msg + '</p>';

});


function sendMessage() {

    var message = document.getElementById('input').value;

    socket.send(message);

    document.getElementById('input').value = '';

}
```
    </script>
</head>
<body>
    <h1>WebSocket with Flask</h1>
    <div id="messages"></div>
    <input type="text" id="input" placeholder="Type a message">
    <button onclick="sendMessage()">Send</button>
</body>
</html>

In this example:

- The client connects to the Flask-SocketIO server via io.connect().
- The socket.on('message') function listens for incoming messages from the server.

- The sendMessage() function sends a message to the server whenever the button is clicked.

Scaling WebSockets with Flask

Flask-SocketIO provides support for scaling WebSocket applications by using message queues and distributed systems like **Redis**. This allows multiple servers to share WebSocket messages, enabling your application to scale horizontally.

To use Redis for scaling:

bash

CopyEdit

```
pip install redis
```

Then, configure Flask-SocketIO to use Redis:

python

CopyEdit

```
app.config['SOCKETIO_MESSAGE_QUEUE'] = 'redis://localhost:6379/0'
```

This configuration allows Flask-SocketIO to use Redis as the message queue for scaling WebSocket connections across multiple application instances.

Conclusion

WebSockets enable real-time communication in Flask applications, making it ideal for interactive features like chat systems, notifications, and live updates. Flask-SocketIO simplifies the integration of WebSockets into Flask by providing an easy-to-use API, and it can scale to handle large numbers of concurrent connections using Redis as a message queue.

9.5 Working with Flask and GraphQL

GraphQL is an API query language that provides a more flexible and efficient way to interact with APIs compared to traditional REST APIs. Unlike REST, where you have to make multiple requests to fetch different types of data, GraphQL allows you to request only the data you need in a single query, reducing the number of round-trips to the server.

Flask doesn't natively support GraphQL, but the **Flask-GraphQL** extension provides a way to integrate GraphQL into your Flask applications easily.

Why Use GraphQL with Flask?

1. **Flexibility**: With GraphQL, clients can specify the structure of the response, eliminating over-fetching or under-fetching of data.
2. **Single Endpoint**: Unlike REST APIs, where each resource has its own endpoint, GraphQL provides a single endpoint for all interactions.
3. **Efficient Data Fetching**: GraphQL allows clients to request exactly the data they need, minimizing the amount of data transferred over the network.

Setting Up Flask-GraphQL

To get started with GraphQL in Flask, you need to install **Flask-GraphQL** and **Graphene**, a Python library for building GraphQL APIs.

bash

CopyEdit

```
pip install flask-graphql graphene
```

1. **Creating a GraphQL Schema**

First, define a GraphQL schema using **Graphene**. A schema is a representation of your data model, including types, queries, and mutations (for writing data).

python

CopyEdit

```python
import graphene

from graphene import ObjectType, String, Schema


class Query(ObjectType):

    hello = String(description="Returns a hello message")


    def resolve_hello(self, info):

        return "Hello, GraphQL!"


schema = Schema(query=Query)
```

In this example, we define a simple Query type with a hello field that returns a greeting message.

2. **Integrating GraphQL with Flask**

Now, integrate **Flask-GraphQL** with your Flask application by providing the schema and defining a route for GraphQL queries.

python

CopyEdit

```python
from flask import Flask

from flask_graphql import GraphQLView


app = Flask(__name__)
```

```
app.add_url_rule(

    '/graphql', view_func=GraphQLView.as_view('graphql', schema=schema,
graphiql=True)

)

if __name__ == '__main__':

    app.run(debug=True)
```

Here:

- We add a /graphql route that serves the GraphQL API.
- graphiql=True enables the interactive GraphiQL interface, where you can manually test GraphQL queries in the browser.
3. **Making a GraphQL Query**

Once your Flask app is running, you can access the GraphiQL interface at http://localhost:5000/graphql in your browser. You can enter the following query:

graphql

CopyEdit

```
{

    hello

}
```

This query will return:

json

CopyEdit

```
{
```

165

```
"data": {

  "hello": "Hello, GraphQL!"

  }

}
```

Best Practices for Using GraphQL in Flask

- **Schema Design**: Start by designing your schema to closely represent your application's data model. Keep your schema flexible and modular.
- **Batch Requests**: Use GraphQL's ability to batch multiple queries in a single request to reduce the number of requests made to the server.
- **Error Handling**: Handle errors carefully in GraphQL, especially when dealing with complex nested queries. GraphQL provides a standard error format that you should use to communicate errors in the response.
- **Authorization**: Implement authorization and authentication in your GraphQL resolvers to ensure only authorized users can query or mutate data.

9.6 Using Flask with Docker for Containerization

Docker is a platform that allows you to package your applications and their dependencies into containers, which are lightweight, portable, and consistent across different environments. Docker is widely used in modern development workflows, enabling easier deployment, scaling, and testing of applications.

Why Use Docker with Flask?

1. **Consistency**: Docker ensures that your Flask application will run the same way in any environment, whether it's development, testing, or production. This eliminates issues with dependency versions and environment mismatches.
2. **Portability**: Docker containers can be deployed anywhere, from local machines to cloud platforms like AWS, Google Cloud, or Azure.
3. **Scalability**: Docker makes it easy to scale your Flask application by running multiple instances of your app in separate containers, allowing for better load distribution.

Setting Up Docker with Flask

1. **Create a Dockerfile**

A Dockerfile is a script that defines how to build a Docker image for your Flask application. Here's an example Dockerfile for a Flask application:

Dockerfile

CopyEdit

```
# Use an official Python runtime as a base image

FROM python:3.9-slim


# Set the working directory inside the container

WORKDIR /app


# Copy the requirements file into the container

COPY requirements.txt .


# Install the dependencies

RUN pip install --no-cache-dir -r requirements.txt


# Copy the application code into the container

COPY . .


# Set the environment variable for Flask
```

167

```
ENV FLASK_APP=app.py

ENV FLASK_RUN_HOST=0.0.0.0


# Expose the port that Flask will run on

EXPOSE 5000


# Run the Flask application

CMD ["flask", "run"]
```

In this Dockerfile:

- We use the official Python 3.9 slim image as the base.
- We set /app as the working directory in the container.
- We copy the requirements.txt file, install the dependencies, and then copy the entire application code into the container.
- We expose port 5000, which is the default port for Flask.
2. **Create a requirements.txt File**

The requirements.txt file should list all the Python packages required by your application, including Flask and any extensions:

nginx

CopyEdit

```
flask

flask-sqlalchemy

flask-restful
```

3. Build the Docker Image

Once the Dockerfile and requirements.txt are set up, build the Docker image:

bash

CopyEdit

```
docker build -t flask-app .
```

4. Run the Docker Container

After building the Docker image, you can run the container:

bash

CopyEdit

```
docker run -p 5000:5000 flask-app
```

This command runs the Flask application inside the container and maps port 5000 on your machine to port 5000 in the container, making the Flask application accessible at http://localhost:5000.

Using Docker Compose for Multi-Container Applications

If your Flask application depends on other services, such as a database, you can use **Docker Compose** to manage multiple containers. Create a docker-compose.yml file:

yaml

CopyEdit

```
version: '3'

services:

  flask-app:
```

```
build: .

ports:

  - "5000:5000"

db:

  image: postgres

  environment:

    POSTGRES_DB: flaskdb

    POSTGRES_USER: user

    POSTGRES_PASSWORD: password
```

With this setup:

- The Flask app and PostgreSQL database run in separate containers.
- Flask connects to the db service using the environment variables provided.

Run the application with:

bash

CopyEdit

```
docker-compose up
```

Chapter 10: Deploying Flask APIs

10.1 Deployment Strategies: Local vs. Cloud

When deploying a Flask API, one of the first decisions you'll need to make is whether to host your application locally (on your own machine or server) or in the cloud. Both options have their advantages and trade-offs, depending on the size of your application, your team's expertise, and the resources available. Understanding the key differences between local and cloud deployments will help you make an informed decision.

Local Deployment

Deploying your Flask API locally means that your application will run on a server that you own or manage, either physically or virtually. Local deployment is commonly used for development, testing, and small-scale production applications.

Advantages of Local Deployment:

1. **Full Control**: You have complete control over the environment, hardware, and configurations. This is particularly beneficial for applications with specific infrastructure requirements.
2. **Cost-Effective for Small Projects**: Local hosting can be more affordable for small projects or during the early stages of development, as you only pay for the resources you own.
3. **No External Dependencies**: By hosting your application locally, you avoid relying on external services like cloud providers, which can introduce complexity or additional costs.

Disadvantages of Local Deployment:

1. **Scalability Challenges**: Scaling a locally hosted Flask API can be difficult, as it requires additional hardware or complex software configurations, such as load balancing and high availability setups.
2. **Limited Accessibility**: A locally hosted application may be harder to access remotely unless you configure public IPs or use VPNs, limiting accessibility.
3. **Maintenance Overhead**: Hosting locally requires ongoing maintenance, including hardware monitoring, backups, security, and updates.

When to Use Local Deployment:

- During development or testing phases.
- For small, non-critical applications or personal projects.
- When the application doesn't need to scale quickly.

Cloud Deployment

Cloud deployment means hosting your Flask API on a cloud platform such as **AWS**, **Google Cloud**, **Microsoft Azure**, or **Heroku**. Cloud hosting allows you to offload the management of hardware and infrastructure, focusing instead on developing and scaling the application.

Advantages of Cloud Deployment:

1. **Scalability**: Cloud platforms offer virtually unlimited resources. As your application grows, you can scale your infrastructure easily with minimal effort, often with just a few clicks or API calls.
2. **High Availability**: Cloud providers offer services like load balancing and multi-region deployments, ensuring your application stays up and responsive even during peak traffic or server failures.
3. **Automation and Tools**: Cloud providers offer a range of tools for monitoring, logging, security, CI/CD pipelines, and automatic scaling, allowing you to focus on development rather than infrastructure.
4. **Global Accessibility**: Cloud applications can be accessed from anywhere, making it easy to serve a global user base.

Disadvantages of Cloud Deployment:

1. **Ongoing Costs**: While cloud services are cost-effective for scaling, they can become expensive over time, especially for high-traffic applications. Pricing models are based on resource usage, so you must carefully manage your consumption.
2. **Dependency on External Providers**: Cloud services can experience outages or service disruptions, which could impact your Flask API's availability, though many providers offer service level agreements (SLAs) to guarantee uptime.
3. **Learning Curve**: Cloud platforms can be complex to configure, especially for those unfamiliar with their services or infrastructure management.

When to Use Cloud Deployment:

- For production applications that need to scale quickly or globally.
- When you need high availability, security, and redundancy.
- For applications with a rapidly changing user base or unpredictable traffic.
- When you prefer to delegate infrastructure management to the cloud provider.

10.2 Deploying Flask to Heroku

Heroku is a platform-as-a-service (PaaS) that allows developers to deploy, manage, and scale web applications in a simple and efficient way. It is particularly popular among developers who want to focus on writing code rather than managing infrastructure. Heroku abstracts away much of the complexity of deployment and offers a streamlined process for deploying Flask applications.

Why Choose Heroku for Flask Deployment?

1. **Ease of Use**: Heroku simplifies deployment by offering a user-friendly interface and simple commands to deploy your application.
2. **Automatic Scaling**: With Heroku, you can scale your application by adjusting the number of dynos (containers) to handle traffic fluctuations.
3. **Built-in Add-ons**: Heroku provides easy integration with numerous add-ons such as databases (PostgreSQL, Redis), caching, monitoring, and more.
4. **Free Tier**: For small applications or prototypes, Heroku offers a free tier with limitations (such as limited dyno hours), making it ideal for developers looking to get started quickly.

Deploying Flask on Heroku: Step-by-Step

1. **Install the Heroku CLI**

To deploy your Flask application on Heroku, you'll need the Heroku Command Line Interface (CLI). Download and install the CLI from the official Heroku website.

bash
CopyEdit
```
# Install the Heroku CLI
https://devcenter.heroku.com/articles/heroku-cli
```

173

2. Create a Heroku Account

Sign up for a Heroku account at https://signup.heroku.com.

3. Prepare Your Flask Application

Before deploying, make sure your Flask application is set up correctly. The basic structure should include:

- app.py (or application.py if using WSGI)
- requirements.txt for dependencies
- Procfile for Heroku to know how to run your app
- runtime.txt (optional) to specify Python version

Example structure:

markdown
CopyEdit
```
my-flask-app/
    ├── app.py
    ├── requirements.txt
    ├── Procfile
    └── runtime.txt
```

4. Create a Procfile

The Procfile tells Heroku how to run your Flask app. This file should contain a line like:

makefile
CopyEdit
```
web: gunicorn app:app
```

- web indicates that Heroku should run a web process.
- gunicorn is the WSGI server used to run Flask in production.
- app:app refers to the app.py file and the Flask app instance inside it.

5. Create a requirements.txt File

Use the following command to generate the requirements.txt file, which lists the dependencies required for your Flask application:

bash
CopyEdit

```
pip freeze > requirements.txt
```

Make sure the requirements.txt includes all the necessary libraries like Flask, gunicorn, and any other dependencies your application uses.

6. Create a runtime.txt File (Optional)

If you want to specify a particular version of Python, create a runtime.txt file with the Python version, such as:

CopyEdit

```
python-3.9.6
```

7. Initialize a Git Repository

Heroku uses Git for deployment, so you need to initialize a Git repository in your Flask project directory:

bash
CopyEdit

```
git init
git add .
git commit -m "Initial commit"
```

8. Log in to Heroku via CLI

Authenticate with your Heroku account:

bash
CopyEdit

```
heroku login
```

9. **Create a Heroku Application**

Create a new Heroku app by running the following command:

```bash
CopyEdit
heroku create my-flask-app
```

This will create a new app on Heroku with a unique URL, such as https://my-flask-app.herokuapp.com.

10. **Deploy Your Flask Application**

Push your Flask app to Heroku using Git:

```bash
CopyEdit
git push heroku master
```

Heroku will automatically detect that it's a Python application, install the required dependencies, and start the web dyno using gunicorn.

11. **Open Your App in the Browser**

Once the deployment is complete, you can open your Flask app in the browser:

```bash
CopyEdit
heroku open
```

This will open the URL of your newly deployed Flask app.

10.3 Configuring Your Flask App for Production

When deploying your Flask API to production, there are several key configuration considerations to ensure that your application performs optimally, is secure, and can handle real-world traffic.

1. Use a Production-Grade WSGI Server (e.g., Gunicorn)

In production, Flask's built-in development server is not suitable for handling real-world traffic. Instead, use a production-grade WSGI server such as **Gunicorn** or **uWSGI**. Gunicorn is a Python WSGI HTTP server for UNIX, and it is widely used in production environments to serve Flask applications.

To install Gunicorn, run:

```bash
CopyEdit
pip install gunicorn
```

Then, update your Procfile to use Gunicorn:

```makefile
CopyEdit
web: gunicorn app:app
```

2. Set DEBUG to False

Flask's DEBUG mode is great for development but should never be enabled in production. Setting DEBUG = False ensures that error messages are not exposed to the client.

In your Flask app configuration:

```python
CopyEdit
app.config['DEBUG'] = False
app.config['ENV'] = 'production'
```

3. Use Environment Variables for Configuration

For security reasons, sensitive information such as database credentials, API keys, and secret keys should not be hardcoded in your application. Instead, use environment variables to store this data.

For example, you can use Python's os module to access environment variables:

```python
CopyEdit
import os

app.config['SECRET_KEY'] = os.getenv('FLASK_SECRET_KEY')
app.config['SQLALCHEMY_DATABASE_URI'] = os.getenv('DATABASE_URL')
```

Set environment variables in your hosting platform or local environment.

4. Enable Logging for Production

Logging is crucial for diagnosing issues and monitoring your application in production. Flask allows you to configure logging using Python's built-in logging module.

Example of configuring logging:

```python
CopyEdit
import logging
from logging.handlers import RotatingFileHandler

if not app.debug:
    handler = RotatingFileHandler('app.log', maxBytes=10000, backupCount=1)
    handler.setLevel(logging.INFO)
    app.logger.addHandler(handler)
```

This configuration sets up rotating logs and ensures that logs are only recorded at the INFO level or higher in production.

5. Use a Reverse Proxy (e.g., Nginx)

In production, Flask should run behind a reverse proxy like **Nginx** or **Apache**. These proxies handle incoming HTTP requests and pass them to the Flask application, providing additional functionality such as load balancing, security, and serving static files.

Configure Nginx to forward requests to Gunicorn:

```nginx
CopyEdit
server {
    listen 80;
    server_name my-flask-app.com;

    location / {
        proxy_pass http://127.0.0.1:8000;
        proxy_set_header Host $host;
        proxy_set_header X-Real-IP $remote_addr;
    }
}
```

6. Enable HTTPS

Ensure that your Flask application is served over HTTPS to encrypt traffic and protect user data. You can enable HTTPS by configuring an SSL/TLS certificate for your domain. Services like **Let's Encrypt** provide free SSL certificates that can be easily integrated with Nginx or Apache.

10.4 Using Docker and Kubernetes for Scalability

As your Flask API grows and handles more traffic, you'll need a scalable and reliable way to manage your application infrastructure. **Docker** and **Kubernetes** provide a powerful solution for containerizing your application and orchestrating the deployment of multiple containers, ensuring that your Flask API can scale efficiently and handle increased traffic.

Why Use Docker and Kubernetes for Scalability?

1. **Docker**: Docker allows you to package your Flask API and its dependencies into isolated containers. This ensures that the application runs consistently across different environments (development, testing, production) and that all dependencies are included within the container.
2. **Kubernetes**: Kubernetes is a container orchestration platform that automates the deployment, scaling, and management of containerized applications. With Kubernetes, you can manage large numbers of containers, monitor their health, and scale your Flask API based on demand.

1. Using Docker for Flask Deployment

To scale your Flask application with Docker, you first need to create a Docker image that contains your application and its dependencies. Here's a quick summary of the process:

Create a Dockerfile:
A Dockerfile defines the environment for your Flask app inside the container. Here's an example:
Dockerfile
CopyEdit

```
# Use an official Python runtime as a base image
FROM python:3.9-slim

# Set the working directory inside the container
WORKDIR /app

# Install dependencies
COPY requirements.txt .
RUN pip install --no-cache-dir -r requirements.txt

# Copy the application code into the container
COPY . .

# Set environment variables
ENV FLASK_APP=app.py
ENV FLASK_RUN_HOST=0.0.0.0
```

```
# Expose port 5000 for the application
EXPOSE 5000

# Run the Flask app with Gunicorn
CMD ["gunicorn", "app:app", "-b", "0.0.0.0:5000"]
```

1. **Build the Docker Image**:
   After creating the Dockerfile, build the image by running:
   bash
   CopyEdit
   ```
   docker build -t flask-api .
   ```

2. **Run the Docker Container**:
   Run the container with:
   bash
   CopyEdit
   ```
   docker run -p 5000:5000 flask-api
   ```

2. Scaling with Kubernetes

Once your Flask app is containerized with Docker, you can use **Kubernetes** to scale it efficiently.

1. **Set Up a Kubernetes Cluster**: You can set up a Kubernetes cluster on cloud platforms like AWS, Google Cloud, or DigitalOcean. Many providers offer managed Kubernetes services (like **Amazon EKS**, **Google Kubernetes Engine**, or **DigitalOcean Kubernetes**) that simplify the cluster setup.

Create Kubernetes Deployment Configuration: Create a Kubernetes deployment configuration file (deployment.yaml) to define how your Flask API will run in the cluster.
yaml
CopyEdit
```
apiVersion: apps/v1
```

181

```
kind: Deployment
metadata:
  name: flask-api-deployment
spec:
  replicas: 3  # Number of replicas (containers)
  selector:
    matchLabels:
      app: flask-api
  template:
    metadata:
      labels:
        app: flask-api
    spec:
      containers:
      - name: flask-api
        image: flask-api:latest  # Replace with your image name
        ports:
        - containerPort: 5000
```

2. Apply the Deployment: Apply the deployment to Kubernetes:
bash
CopyEdit
```
kubectl apply -f deployment.yaml
```

3. Scaling the Application: To scale the application (increase or decrease the number of containers), you can modify the replicas field in the deployment.yaml file or run the following command:
bash
CopyEdit
```
kubectl scale deployment flask-api-deployment --replicas=5
```

Expose the Flask Application: Create a service to expose your Flask application to the outside world:

182

yaml
CopyEdit

```yaml
apiVersion: v1
kind: Service
metadata:
  name: flask-api-service
spec:
  selector:
    app: flask-api
  ports:
    - protocol: TCP
      port: 80
      targetPort: 5000
  type: LoadBalancer
```

Apply the service:

bash
CopyEdit

```bash
kubectl apply -f service.yaml
```

By using **Docker** and **Kubernetes**, you can easily scale your Flask API by adjusting the number of replicas, balancing traffic across multiple containers, and ensuring high availability and fault tolerance.

10.5 Setting Up Continuous Integration/Continuous Deployment (CI/CD)

Continuous Integration (CI) and **Continuous Deployment (CD)** are essential practices for modern application development. CI involves automatically integrating code changes into a shared repository, while CD automates the process of deploying code changes to production. Setting up CI/CD pipelines for your Flask API allows you to automatically test, build, and deploy your application with minimal manual intervention.

Why Use CI/CD?

1. **Automated Testing**: CI/CD ensures that tests are run automatically whenever new code is pushed, reducing the chances of bugs and errors in production.
2. **Faster Development Cycles**: CI/CD speeds up the development cycle by automating manual steps such as code integration, testing, and deployment.
3. **Consistent Deployment**: CI/CD ensures that every deployment is consistent and reproducible, minimizing the risk of human error during deployment.

Setting Up CI/CD for Flask

Here's how to set up CI/CD for your Flask application using popular tools like **GitHub Actions** and **CircleCI**.

1. **GitHub Actions for CI/CD**

GitHub Actions allows you to automate workflows directly in your GitHub repository. Here's how to create a simple CI/CD pipeline for Flask using GitHub Actions.

Create a .github/workflows/ci-cd.yaml **File**: This file defines the steps for CI/CD. It will install dependencies, run tests, build the Docker image, and deploy the Flask API to your server.
yaml
CopyEdit

```
name: Flask CI/CD Pipeline

on:
  push:
    branches:
      - main

jobs:
  build:
    runs-on: ubuntu-latest

    steps:
      - name: Checkout repository
        uses: actions/checkout@v2
```

```yaml
- name: Set up Python
  uses: actions/setup-python@v2
  with:
    python-version: 3.9

- name: Install dependencies
  run: |
    pip install -r requirements.txt

- name: Run tests
  run: |
    pytest

- name: Build Docker image
  run: |
    docker build -t flask-api .

- name: Push Docker image
  run: |
    docker push your-docker-repo/flask-api

- name: Deploy to server (example with SSH)
  uses: appleboy/ssh-action@v0.1.4
  with:
    host: ${{ secrets.HOST }}
    username: ${{ secrets.USERNAME }}
    key: ${{ secrets.SSH_PRIVATE_KEY }}
    script: |
      docker pull your-docker-repo/flask-api
      docker run -d -p 5000:5000 your-docker-repo/flask-api
```

1. **Set Secrets for Deployment**: Add secrets for your deployment, such as the server's host, username, and SSH private key, in your GitHub repository's settings under **Secrets**.
2. **Push to GitHub**: When you push changes to the main branch, GitHub Actions will automatically run the CI/CD pipeline, which installs dependencies, runs tests, builds the Docker image, and deploys the app to your server.

3. CircleCI for CI/CD

CircleCI is another popular CI/CD tool that integrates well with Flask applications. Here's how to set up a CircleCI pipeline.

Create a .circleci/config.yml **File**: This file defines the steps for testing, building, and deploying your Flask API.
yaml
CopyEdit

```yaml
version: 2.1

jobs:
  build:
    docker:
      - image: circleci/python:3.9
    steps:
      - checkout
      - run:
          name: Install dependencies
          command: pip install -r requirements.txt
      - run:
          name: Run tests
          command: pytest
      - run:
          name: Build Docker image
          command: docker build -t flask-api .
      - run:
          name: Push Docker image
          command: docker push your-docker-repo/flask-api

  deploy:
    docker:
      - image: circleci/python:3.9
    steps:
      - checkout
      - run:
          name: Deploy to server (example with SSH)
          command: |
```

186

```
docker pull your-docker-repo/flask-api
docker run -d -p 5000:5000 your-docker-repo/flask-api
```

```
workflows:
 version: 2
 deploy:
  jobs:
    - build
    - deploy:
       requires:
        - build
```

1. **Set Environment Variables**: In CircleCI, you can store sensitive information such as API keys and deployment credentials as environment variables to keep them secure.

10.6 Deploying Flask on AWS or DigitalOcean

Both **AWS** and **DigitalOcean** are powerful cloud platforms that can be used to deploy Flask APIs. Both services offer flexible and scalable solutions, but the choice between them depends on your requirements, budget, and experience.

Deploying Flask on AWS

1. **Set Up an EC2 Instance**:
    o Launch an EC2 instance (Amazon's virtual server) and select an appropriate AMI (Amazon Machine Image).
    o SSH into your EC2 instance and install necessary dependencies like Python, Flask, and Gunicorn.
    o Use AWS Elastic Load Balancer (ELB) to distribute incoming traffic across multiple EC2 instances for scalability.
2. **Set Up RDS for Database**:
    o Use **Amazon RDS** (Relational Database Service) to host your database (e.g., MySQL, PostgreSQL) and connect it to your Flask app.
3. **Configure S3 for Static File Hosting**:
    o For hosting static files like images, use **Amazon S3** (Simple Storage Service) to manage and serve assets.

Deploying Flask on DigitalOcean

1. **Create a Droplet**:
   - ○ DigitalOcean's virtual servers, called Droplets, can be quickly provisioned. Choose the appropriate plan and OS image.
   - ○ Install Flask, Gunicorn, and Nginx on your Droplet.
2. **Set Up Managed Databases**:
   - ○ Use **DigitalOcean Managed Databases** for PostgreSQL or MySQL to simplify database management.
3. **Using Spaces for Static File Hosting**:
   - ○ DigitalOcean Spaces is a great alternative to Amazon S3 for serving static files.

0.7 Monitoring and Logging Flask APIs in Production

Monitoring and logging are critical components of maintaining a Flask API in production. Effective monitoring helps identify performance issues and errors before they impact users, while logging provides valuable insights into the application's behavior and errors.

Monitoring Flask APIs

1. **Use Cloud Monitoring Services**:
   - ○ AWS offers **CloudWatch**, and DigitalOcean provides **Monitoring** services that allow you to track CPU usage, memory usage, disk I/O, and network traffic for your application.
   - ○ **New Relic** and **Datadog** are popular third-party monitoring services that provide in-depth performance metrics, including response times, error rates, and application throughput.
2. **Application Performance Monitoring (APM)**:
   - ○ Tools like **Sentry** and **Rollbar** can be integrated with your Flask app to capture and report errors in real-time.
3. **Custom Metrics with Prometheus**:
   - ○ **Prometheus** is a powerful open-source tool for collecting and querying time-series data. Flask applications can expose custom metrics through HTTP endpoints, and Prometheus can scrape those metrics for analysis.

Logging Flask APIs

1. **Flask's Built-in Logging**:
   - Flask integrates with Python's standard logging module, which allows you to log application activity, errors, and other important events. Configure logging to write logs to a file or external logging service.
2. **Third-Party Logging Services**:
   - **Loggly**, **Papertrail**, and **Splunk** are third-party services that provide centralized logging, making it easy to aggregate and analyze logs from multiple sources.
3. **Structured Logging**:
   - Use **JSON** or **key-value pairs** for structured logging, which makes it easier to analyze and filter logs programmatically.

Effective monitoring and logging are vital for identifying performance issues and errors in Flask APIs in production. By using cloud services like CloudWatch, third-party APM tools, and integrating structured logging into your Flask application, you can ensure that your API remains performant, reliable, and easy to troubleshoot.

Chapter 11: Documentation and API Versioning

11.1 The Importance of API Documentation

When developing an API, one of the most crucial aspects often overlooked is **documentation**. Well-documented APIs are essential for both users and developers, ensuring that the API is easy to understand, use, and maintain. API documentation is not only beneficial for external developers who integrate with your API but also for your team members who will be working with the API in the future.

Why Is API Documentation Important?

1. **Ease of Use**: Comprehensive and clear documentation helps developers understand how to interact with your API. It provides the necessary information on endpoints, request parameters, response formats, and error codes.
2. **Consistency**: Documentation ensures that developers follow consistent patterns when using the API. This reduces confusion and promotes standardization, especially when multiple teams are involved.
3. **Reduces Errors and Misuse**: Good documentation minimizes the chances of developers misusing the API or making mistakes due to a lack of information. It highlights edge cases, requirements, and constraints for every endpoint.
4. **Faster Onboarding**: For new developers or external teams, clear API documentation serves as a tutorial or guide, helping them get up to speed quickly without needing to ask a lot of questions.
5. **Client Collaboration**: Clients (other teams, partners, or third-party developers) often rely on API documentation to integrate your API into their systems. The clearer and more comprehensive your documentation is, the faster they can start working with your API.
6. **Maintainability**: As your API evolves, having up-to-date documentation makes it easier to manage changes and updates. This ensures that any new developers or collaborators can easily understand the structure of your API.

Components of Good API Documentation

A well-structured API documentation includes the following key components:

- **Introduction**: A brief description of what the API does and its primary use cases.
- **Authentication and Authorization**: Explanation of how clients can authenticate and access the API (e.g., via API keys, OAuth, JWT).
- **Endpoint Descriptions**: Detailed descriptions of each API endpoint, including the method (GET, POST, PUT, DELETE), required parameters, and the format of the request and response.
- **Request and Response Examples**: Providing example payloads for both requests and responses helps developers understand the data format.
- **Error Codes and Messages**: A list of possible error codes and what they mean helps users diagnose issues when interacting with the API.
- **Rate Limiting**: Information on rate limits and any restrictions on the number of requests a client can make to avoid overloading the server.

The Cost of Poor Documentation

Without proper documentation, your API risks becoming a barrier to adoption. Clients will struggle to understand how to use it effectively, leading to frustration, errors, and ultimately, a lack of interest in integrating with it. In the worst case, poor documentation can lead to abandoned integrations, stalled development, and negative feedback from users.

11.2 Using Swagger (OpenAPI) to Document APIs

Swagger, now known as **OpenAPI**, is a widely adopted framework for describing RESTful APIs. It provides a standardized way to define your API's structure and behavior. Swagger enables the automatic generation of API documentation, client libraries, and even server stubs, making the API development and integration process much easier.

What is OpenAPI (Swagger)?

OpenAPI (formerly Swagger) is a specification for describing APIs in a language-agnostic format. It allows you to define your API endpoints, request/response formats, authentication methods, and more. This specification serves as a blueprint for both human readers and machines, enabling tools to generate API documentation and code.

OpenAPI follows a structured format, usually written in **YAML** or **JSON**, to describe the API's endpoints and their expected inputs and outputs.

Advantages of Using Swagger (OpenAPI)

1. **Standardization**: OpenAPI provides a standardized way to describe RESTful APIs, ensuring that the API description is consistent and well-organized.
2. **Interactive Documentation**: Tools like **Swagger UI** allow you to present your API documentation in an interactive, user-friendly interface where developers can test endpoints directly from the browser.
3. **Automatic Code Generation**: OpenAPI allows the automatic generation of client libraries, server stubs, and even API tests, saving developers time and reducing errors.
4. **Machine-Readable Format**: Since OpenAPI is machine-readable, it can be used for automated documentation generation, validation, and integration into CI/CD pipelines.
5. **Supports Multiple Languages**: Swagger/OpenAPI works with various programming languages and frameworks, making it a versatile tool for API development.

How to Use OpenAPI (Swagger) with Flask

To use Swagger/OpenAPI in a Flask application, you can integrate it using libraries such as **Flask-RESTPlus**, **Flask-Swagger-UI**, or **Flask-OpenAPI**. These libraries simplify the integration of OpenAPI specifications and automatically generate interactive documentation.

Here's how to set up Swagger documentation with Flask-RESTPlus, which integrates the OpenAPI specification into your Flask application.

1. **Install Flask-RESTPlus**:

bash
CopyEdit
```
pip install flask-restplus
```

2. Define Your API Using Flask-RESTPlus:

```python
CopyEdit
from flask import Flask
from flask_restplus import Api, Resource

app = Flask(__name__)
api = Api(app, version='1.0', title='Flask API', description='A simple Flask API with Swagger documentation')

@api.route('/hello')
class HelloWorld(Resource):
    def get(self):
        """
        A simple GET endpoint that returns a greeting.
        ---
        responses:
          200:
            description: A greeting message
            examples:
              application/json: {"message": "Hello, World!"}
        """
        return {'message': 'Hello, World!'}

if __name__ == '__main__':
    app.run(debug=True)
```

In this example:

- We define a Flask app and set up Swagger/OpenAPI documentation using **Flask-RESTPlus**.
- The @api.route() decorator defines a new endpoint (/hello).
- The get() method handles GET requests for that endpoint and includes an OpenAPI-compliant docstring explaining the response structure.
3. **Accessing the Swagger UI**: When you run the app, Swagger UI will automatically generate interactive documentation at http://localhost:5000/.

11.3 Flask-RESTPlus for Automatic API Docs

Flask-RESTPlus is an extension for Flask that helps you build REST APIs quickly and easily. It integrates with **Swagger (OpenAPI)** to automatically generate API documentation, reducing the manual work involved in documenting each endpoint.

Why Use Flask-RESTPlus?

1. **Automatic Documentation**: Flask-RESTPlus automatically generates Swagger-based API documentation, which can be easily accessed via a web interface.
2. **Structured Request and Response Handling**: It provides tools for defining and validating input and output formats, ensuring that the API adheres to a consistent structure.
3. **Enhanced Error Handling**: Flask-RESTPlus offers built-in error handling mechanisms that make it easier to manage HTTP errors and send meaningful responses.
4. **Input Validation**: It includes tools for validating request data (e.g., JSON payloads) to ensure they meet the expected schema, reducing errors and improving the robustness of the API.
5. **Namespace Organization**: Flask-RESTPlus allows you to organize your API into namespaces, making it easier to structure large applications with multiple endpoints.

Setting Up Flask-RESTPlus for API Docs

1. **Installation**:

To use Flask-RESTPlus, you need to install the package:

```bash
CopyEdit
pip install flask-restplus
```

2. **Create a Flask-RESTPlus API**:

```python
CopyEdit
from flask import Flask
```

194

```python
from flask_restplus import Api, Resource, fields

app = Flask(__name__)
api = Api(app, version='1.0', title='Flask-RESTPlus API', description='An API with
automatic documentation')

# Define a model for input data
todo = api.model('Todo', {
    'task': fields.String(required=True, description='The task to be done')
})

# Define the API endpoint
@api.route('/todos')
class TodoList(Resource):
    def get(self):
        """
        Get a list of tasks
        ---
        responses:
          200:
            description: A list of tasks
            examples:
                application/json: [{"task": "Do the laundry"}]
        """
        return [{'task': 'Do the laundry'}, {'task': 'Go shopping'}]

    @api.expect(todo)
    def post(self):
        """
        Create a new task
        ---
        responses:
          201:
            description: Task created
        """
        return {'task': 'New Task Created'}, 201

if __name__ == '__main__':
```

```
app.run(debug=True)
```

In this example:

- We use **Flask-RESTPlus** to define a simple API for managing tasks (/todos endpoint).
- The api.model() method defines a data model (todo) for validating incoming requests.
- The @api.route() decorator creates the /todos endpoint, with GET and POST methods.
- Swagger-compatible docstrings (---) provide the API description, request parameters, and responses.
3. **Accessing the Documentation**: Flask-RESTPlus will automatically generate Swagger UI at the /swagger endpoint, making it easy to test and interact with your API directly from the browser.

11.4 Managing API Versions

As your Flask API evolves over time, managing different versions becomes crucial. API versioning ensures that older clients continue to work without disruption, even as new features and changes are introduced. Proper API versioning helps maintain backward compatibility and provides a clear upgrade path for consumers of your API.

Why API Versioning is Important

1. **Backward Compatibility**: New versions of your API may introduce breaking changes, such as removing or altering endpoints. Versioning allows you to introduce new features without breaking existing functionality for current users.
2. **Client Flexibility**: Clients can choose which version of the API to use based on their needs. This gives clients control over when they decide to upgrade.
3. **Clear Communication**: Versioning communicates to consumers that there are new changes to the API and that they should upgrade to take advantage of new features, fixes, or improvements.

Types of API Versioning

There are several common strategies for versioning an API, each with its advantages and disadvantages. The most widely used methods are:

URI Versioning (Path Versioning): This is the most straightforward approach, where the version number is included directly in the URL path. It's easy to implement and clearly communicates the version of the API that's being accessed.
Example:
bash
CopyEdit
/api/v1/resource
/api/v2/resource

1. **Pros**:
   - Simple and intuitive.
   - Easy to implement in Flask routes.
2. **Cons**:
   - Requires updates to URLs when changing versions, which may cause issues with old clients if not properly handled.

Implementation in Flask:
python
CopyEdit
```
@app.route('/api/v1/resource')
def get_resource_v1():
    return jsonify({"message": "Version 1 resource"})

@app.route('/api/v2/resource')
def get_resource_v2():
    return jsonify({"message": "Version 2 resource"})
```

Query Parameter Versioning: In this approach, the version is passed as a query parameter. This is useful for cases where you don't want to change the URL structure but still need to distinguish between versions.
Example:
bash
CopyEdit
/api/resource?version=1
/api/resource?version=2

3. **Pros**:
   - Doesn't require URL changes, making it less disruptive for existing clients.
4. **Cons**:
   - The version is less visible in the URL, which may cause confusion.
   - Clients may forget to include the version parameter.

Implementation in Flask:
python
CopyEdit
```
@app.route('/api/resource')
def get_resource():
    version = request.args.get('version', default='1')
    if version == '2':
        return jsonify({"message": "Version 2 resource"})
    return jsonify({"message": "Version 1 resource"})
```

Header Versioning: API versioning can also be done through HTTP headers. This method is useful for cases where you want to keep the URLs clean while still being able to manage versions. It is commonly used with RESTful APIs to maintain separation between the URI and versioning logic.

Example:
bash
CopyEdit
```
GET /api/resource
Headers: {"API-Version": "1"}
```

5. **Pros**:
   - Keeps the URL clean.
   - No need to expose version information in the URL.
6. **Cons**:
   - Requires clients to modify headers, which might not be intuitive.
   - Difficult to test via a web browser (since browsers don't expose HTTP headers).

Implementation in Flask:
python

CopyEdit

```
from flask import request

@app.route('/api/resource')
def get_resource():
    api_version = request.headers.get('API-Version', '1')
    if api_version == '2':
        return jsonify({"message": "Version 2 resource"})
    return jsonify({"message": "Version 1 resource"})
```

Content Negotiation: Another advanced method is to use content negotiation, which involves using the Accept header to specify the desired version of the API. This is particularly useful in RESTful services where the response type may vary (e.g., JSON, XML).
Example:
bash
CopyEdit

```
Accept: application/vnd.myapi.v1+json
```

7. **Pros**:
    o   Keeps URLs clean.
    o   Flexibility to add additional media types (e.g., XML, JSON).
8. **Cons**:
    o   More complex for clients to implement.
    o   Clients must manage content types correctly.

Implementation in Flask:
python
CopyEdit

```
from flask import request

@app.route('/api/resource')
def get_resource():
    accept_header = request.headers.get('Accept', 'application/json')
    if 'v1' in accept_header:
        return jsonify({"message": "Version 1 resource"})
    elif 'v2' in accept_header:
```

199

```
return jsonify({"message": "Version 2 resource"})
return jsonify({"message": "Default version"})
```

Best Practices for API Versioning

- **Use Clear and Consistent Naming**: Make sure your versioning strategy is consistent across the API and easily understandable.
- **Deprecation Policy**: When introducing a new version, consider marking older versions as deprecated. Provide users with ample notice before discontinuing support for old versions.
- **Versioned Documentation**: Maintain version-specific documentation to guide developers through each API version's features and differences.

11.5 Creating an API Documentation Strategy for Your API

Creating a solid API documentation strategy is essential to ensuring that your API is easy to use, consistent, and maintainable. A well-thought-out documentation strategy helps developers understand your API's functionality and how to interact with it effectively, improving adoption and reducing errors.

Key Elements of an API Documentation Strategy

1. **Define the Audience**: Determine who will be using the documentation. Will it be used by internal developers, third-party integrators, or public users? Tailoring the documentation to the audience ensures that it provides the right level of detail and guidance.
2. **Standardize the Documentation Format**: Choose a consistent format for your API documentation. This could be a combination of:
   - **Swagger/OpenAPI**: Provides a standardized way to document RESTful APIs.
   - **Markdown Files**: Simple and easy-to-update format for text-based documentation.
   - **Static Site Generators**: Tools like **MkDocs** or **Docusaurus** that can generate static API documentation from markdown files.
3. **Provide Comprehensive Endpoint Documentation**: For each API endpoint, include the following details:

- URL: The full URL of the endpoint.
- HTTP Method: GET, POST, PUT, DELETE, etc.
- Parameters: A list of query parameters, path variables, and body data.
- Request Body: The format and example payload for POST, PUT, or PATCH requests.
- Response: Example responses, including status codes and JSON structure.
- Error Codes: A list of common error codes (e.g., 400, 404, 500) and their meanings.

4. Version Control: Version your documentation to correspond with different API versions. This helps ensure that users of older versions have access to the correct documentation while new users can access the most up-to-date information.

5. Interactive Documentation: Consider providing interactive API documentation, such as Swagger UI or Redoc, to allow developers to test API endpoints directly from the browser.

6. Authentication & Authorization: Provide clear instructions on how users can authenticate with your API, whether through API keys, OAuth, JWT, or another mechanism.

7. Error Handling and Debugging: Document the common errors users might encounter and provide troubleshooting tips. This could include:
   - Common HTTP errors (e.g., 400, 404, 500).
   - Error response examples: Provide JSON structures for error messages.
   - Possible causes and solutions: Help users understand what might be wrong and how to fix it.

Tips for Writing API Documentation

- Clarity and Simplicity: Avoid jargon and ensure that the documentation is easy to read. Use examples to clarify complex concepts.
- Consistency: Keep naming conventions, formatting, and structure consistent across all documentation.
- Searchability: Make it easy for users to search for specific endpoints, terms, or error codes.

11.6 Generating and Publishing API Documentation

Generating and publishing API documentation allows users to easily access and understand how to interact with your API. Well-documented APIs can significantly improve adoption, reduce developer frustration, and accelerate the integration process.

Automated Documentation Generation

One of the best ways to generate API documentation is to use automated tools like **Swagger/OpenAPI**, which allow you to describe your API using structured specifications (YAML or JSON). Once your API is described, you can automatically generate interactive, user-friendly documentation.

Steps to Generate and Publish API Documentation

Use Swagger/OpenAPI for Automatic Documentation: As discussed in previous sections, Swagger/OpenAPI allows you to define your API and automatically generate interactive documentation.

Tools like **Swagger UI** and **Redoc** can be used to visualize the OpenAPI specification and provide an interactive interface to explore and test the API.

Example:

bash

CopyEdit

```
swagger-cli bundle swagger.yaml -o dist/swagger.json
```

1. **Publish the Documentation**: Once you have generated the API documentation, the next step is to publish it so that users can access it.
   - **Static Hosting**: You can host your API documentation as static files on a web server or a platform like **GitHub Pages**.
   - **API Gateway Integration**: Many API gateways (e.g., **Amazon API Gateway**, **Kong**) allow you to integrate Swagger/OpenAPI documentation directly, so it is published and accessible with your deployed API.
2. **Version Control**: When you deploy new versions of your API, update the documentation to reflect the changes. Use version control (such as Git) to manage the documentation and ensure it stays aligned with your API versions.
3. **Host Interactive Documentation**:
   - **Swagger UI**: A popular open-source project that provides an interactive UI for exploring and testing API endpoints.

- **Redoc**: Another powerful tool for rendering OpenAPI documentation in a user-friendly way.

Best Practices for API Documentation Publishing

1. **Host Documentation Alongside the API**: Publish your documentation on the same domain as the API, ideally within the same URL structure (e.g., /docs or /swagger).
2. **Keep Documentation Up-to-Date**: Ensure your documentation is kept in sync with the API. Any changes to the API (e.g., new endpoints, parameter changes) should be reflected in the documentation immediately.
3. **Use Versioning**: Just like your API, documentation should be versioned. Ensure that users can access documentation that corresponds to the version of the API they are using.

Chapter 12: Flask in the Real World

12.1 Case Studies: Flask in E-Commerce

Flask has proven to be an excellent choice for building web applications across various industries, and one area where it has gained significant traction is in **e-commerce**. Flask's simplicity, flexibility, and scalability make it well-suited for developing dynamic e-commerce platforms. Whether it's building custom product management systems, user authentication, payment processing, or managing inventory, Flask offers the tools needed to create an efficient e-commerce site.

Why Flask for E-Commerce?

1. **Flexibility**: Flask provides the flexibility to structure your application as needed, which is crucial for e-commerce sites where unique workflows and business logic are common.
2. **Lightweight and Fast**: As a micro-framework, Flask allows you to quickly develop and deploy e-commerce sites. It does not come with unnecessary overhead, making it fast and efficient.
3. **Modularity**: Flask's modular architecture allows developers to pick and choose the libraries and components they need, resulting in an application that is tailored to the e-commerce platform's requirements.
4. **Ease of Integration**: Flask integrates seamlessly with various databases, payment gateways, shipping APIs, and other third-party services, which are often essential for e-commerce websites.

Case Study 1: Building a Custom E-Commerce Store with Flask

Let's look at a hypothetical case study of a custom e-commerce store built using Flask. The goal is to build an online store that offers a range of products, integrates with a payment gateway for processing transactions, and provides an administrative dashboard for managing products and orders.

Key Features:

- **Product Management**: Admins can add, update, and delete products through a simple admin interface.
- **User Authentication**: Users can register, log in, and securely handle their personal information using **Flask-Login**.

- **Shopping Cart**: Users can browse products and add them to a shopping cart, which is stored in the session.
- **Payment Integration**: Integration with Stripe or PayPal for processing transactions.
- **Order Management**: Admins can view orders and update order statuses.

Example Code for Product Management:

python
CopyEdit
```python
from flask import Flask, render_template, request, redirect, url_for
from flask_sqlalchemy import SQLAlchemy

app = Flask(__name__)
app.config['SQLALCHEMY_DATABASE_URI'] = 'sqlite:///store.db'
app.config['SECRET_KEY'] = 'mysecret'
db = SQLAlchemy(app)

class Product(db.Model):
    id = db.Column(db.Integer, primary_key=True)
    name = db.Column(db.String(100), nullable=False)
    price = db.Column(db.Float, nullable=False)
    description = db.Column(db.String(500), nullable=False)

@app.route('/add-product', methods=['GET', 'POST'])
def add_product():
    if request.method == 'POST':
        name = request.form['name']
        price = request.form['price']
        description = request.form['description']

        new_product = Product(name=name, price=price, description=description)
        db.session.add(new_product)
        db.session.commit()
        return redirect(url_for('home'))

    return render_template('add_product.html')
```

```
@app.route('/')
def home():
    products = Product.query.all()
    return render_template('home.html', products=products)

if __name__ == "__main__":
    db.create_all()
    app.run(debug=True)
```

In this example:

- We define a Product model using SQLAlchemy to represent products in the database.
- We create a simple form for adding products, which allows admins to enter product details and save them to the database.

Case Study 2: Using Flask for a Marketplace Platform

A marketplace platform where third-party sellers can list their products, and buyers can browse, select, and purchase items is another example of Flask's capabilities in e-commerce.

Key Features:

- **Multi-Vendor Support**: Each vendor has a storefront with their products.
- **Order Fulfillment**: After a customer places an order, the vendor can fulfill the order by updating its status.
- **Search Functionality**: A powerful search engine for users to filter products based on category, price, and other parameters.
- **Real-time Updates**: Vendors and customers can receive real-time notifications when an order is placed, shipped, or delivered.

In this case, Flask's ability to handle both the backend and frontend, along with its strong support for RESTful APIs, makes it a solid choice for building the core of such a platform.

12.2 Building APIs for Mobile Applications

Flask is often used as the backend server for mobile applications. Many mobile applications require a backend API to handle tasks such as user authentication, data storage, and real-time communication. Flask is an excellent choice for building these APIs due to its simplicity and ability to scale as needed.

Why Flask for Mobile App Backends?

1. **Quick API Development**: Flask's minimalistic design allows developers to quickly build RESTful APIs for mobile applications. Its flexibility means that you can integrate it easily with databases, third-party services, and authentication systems.
2. **JSON Support**: Flask supports JSON out-of-the-box, making it ideal for mobile apps that rely heavily on JSON for communication between the frontend (mobile) and backend (Flask).
3. **Database Integration**: Flask works seamlessly with SQLAlchemy or other ORMs to manage data storage for mobile applications, whether it's user profiles, app content, or transaction data.
4. **Authentication**: Flask's integration with JWT (JSON Web Tokens) or OAuth allows secure user authentication for mobile apps, which is crucial for maintaining user privacy and security.

Case Study: Building an API for a Mobile To-Do List App

Consider a mobile To-Do list application that allows users to create, update, and delete tasks. The mobile frontend interacts with a Flask API to perform these operations, while the backend manages the tasks stored in a database.

Key Features:

- **User Authentication**: Users can sign up, log in, and manage their tasks securely using tokens (JWT or OAuth).
- **CRUD Operations**: The mobile app can perform Create, Read, Update, and Delete operations on tasks via API endpoints.
- **Real-time Sync**: As users update their tasks, these changes are reflected across all devices through real-time synchronization (using WebSockets or a background task like Celery).

Example Code for Mobile App API in Flask:

python
CopyEdit
```
from flask import Flask, jsonify, request
from flask_sqlalchemy import SQLAlchemy
from flask_jwt_extended import JWTManager, jwt_required, create_access_token

app = Flask(__name__)
app.config['SQLALCHEMY_DATABASE_URI'] = 'sqlite:///tasks.db'
app.config['SECRET_KEY'] = 'supersecretkey'
app.config['JWT_SECRET_KEY'] = 'jwtsecretkey'

db = SQLAlchemy(app)
jwt = JWTManager(app)

class Task(db.Model):
    id = db.Column(db.Integer, primary_key=True)
    title = db.Column(db.String(100), nullable=False)
    description = db.Column(db.String(500), nullable=True)
    done = db.Column(db.Boolean, default=False)

@app.route('/login', methods=['POST'])
def login():
    username = request.json.get('username', None)
    password = request.json.get('password', None)
    if username == 'user' and password == 'password':  # In a real app, use proper
authentication
        access_token = create_access_token(identity=username)
        return jsonify(access_token=access_token)
    return jsonify(message="Invalid credentials"), 401

@app.route('/tasks', methods=['GET'])
@jwt_required()
def get_tasks():
    tasks = Task.query.all()
    return jsonify([task.title for task in tasks])
```

```
@app.route('/task', methods=['POST'])
@jwt_required()
def add_task():
    title = request.json.get('title', None)
    description = request.json.get('description', None)
    new_task = Task(title=title, description=description)
    db.session.add(new_task)
    db.session.commit()
    return jsonify(message="Task added"), 201

if __name__ == '__main__':
    app.run(debug=True)
```

In this example:

- We use **Flask-JWT-Extended** to handle JWT-based authentication for mobile clients.
- The /tasks endpoint allows users to retrieve their tasks, while the /task endpoint lets them add a new task to the database.
- JWT tokens are required to interact with the endpoints, ensuring secure access.

12.3 Flask for IoT (Internet of Things) Applications

The **Internet of Things (IoT)** refers to the growing network of physical devices that are interconnected through the internet, allowing them to collect and exchange data. Flask is often used as the backend solution for IoT applications because it can easily handle HTTP requests, manage data from various devices, and expose RESTful APIs for communication.

Why Flask for IoT?

1. **Lightweight and Efficient**: Flask's minimalism allows it to handle requests efficiently, which is crucial when dealing with IoT devices that send frequent, small amounts of data.
2. **Integration with IoT Protocols**: Flask can be easily integrated with IoT protocols such as HTTP, MQTT, and CoAP, which are often used for device communication.

3. **Real-time Data Processing**: Flask can be used in combination with WebSockets or Celery to process real-time data from IoT devices, such as sensors or smart appliances.
4. **Database Integration**: Flask works seamlessly with databases like **MongoDB** or **InfluxDB**, which are popular choices for storing time-series data from IoT sensors.

Case Study: Flask for Smart Home IoT Platform

Consider a smart home platform that connects various IoT devices like lights, thermostats, and security cameras. Flask is used as the backend to manage the devices, handle incoming data, and provide real-time status updates to the mobile or web frontend.

Key Features:

- **Device Management**: Users can register, configure, and control IoT devices (e.g., turn on/off lights, adjust thermostat settings).
- **Real-time Data**: The platform can receive and display real-time data from sensors (e.g., temperature readings).
- **Notifications**: The system can send notifications if an anomaly is detected (e.g., high temperature, motion detected).

Example Code for IoT Device Management API:

python
CopyEdit
```python
from flask import Flask, jsonify, request
from flask_socketio import SocketIO

app = Flask(__name__)
socketio = SocketIO(app)

devices = []

@app.route('/register_device', methods=['POST'])
def register_device():
    device_data = request.json
    device_id = device_data['device_id']
```

```
    device_name = device_data['device_name']
    devices.append({'device_id': device_id, 'device_name': device_name})
    return jsonify({"message": "Device registered successfully"}), 201

@app.route('/get_devices', methods=['GET'])
def get_devices():
    return jsonify(devices)

@app.route('/update_device/<device_id>', methods=['POST'])
def update_device(device_id):
    device = next((d for d in devices if d['device_id'] == device_id), None)
    if device:
        status = request.json.get('status')
        socketio.emit(f'device_update_{device_id}', {'status': status})
        return jsonify({"message": "Device status updated"}), 200
    return jsonify({"message": "Device not found"}), 404

if __name__ == '__main__':
    socketio.run(app)
```

In this example:

- Users can register IoT devices via the /register_device endpoint.
- The /get_devices endpoint returns a list of registered devices.
- The /update_device/<device_id> endpoint updates the device's status and broadcasts the status change using **SocketIO** for real-time notifications.

Flask's flexibility and scalability make it an ideal solution for building real-world applications across a variety of domains. From e-commerce platforms to mobile apps and IoT devices, Flask provides the tools needed to develop powerful, efficient, and easy-to-maintain backend systems. By leveraging Flask's simplicity and robust ecosystem, developers can quickly bring their ideas to life and build applications that scale with their needs.

12.4 Building Scalable Flask APIs for Enterprises

In enterprise applications, scalability is one of the most critical requirements. Large-scale systems, with high user volumes and complex functionalities, demand robust backend APIs that can efficiently handle heavy loads, high concurrency, and complex business logic. Flask, despite being a micro-framework, can serve as the backbone for such applications if built properly. With the right architecture, deployment strategies, and optimizations, Flask can handle the demands of enterprise-scale systems.

Challenges in Building Scalable Flask APIs

When scaling a Flask API for enterprise applications, you need to address various challenges, including:

- **High Traffic Load**: Handling thousands (or even millions) of API requests per minute.
- **Concurrency**: Managing concurrent requests from multiple clients, ensuring that each request is processed efficiently.
- **Fault Tolerance**: Ensuring the system remains operational even when parts of it fail.
- **Data Consistency**: Managing large volumes of data and ensuring that data remains consistent across different parts of the system.
- **Latency**: Minimizing delays in processing requests, particularly for real-time applications.

Best Practices for Building Scalable Flask APIs

Use a Production-Grade WSGI Server: Flask's development server is not designed for production. For handling high traffic, use a production-grade WSGI server like **Gunicorn** or **uWSGI**. These servers are capable of handling multiple worker processes, allowing Flask to serve requests in parallel and improving the overall throughput. Example with Gunicorn:

bash
CopyEdit
```
gunicorn -w 4 myapp:app
```

This starts 4 worker processes to handle incoming requests concurrently.

1. **Caching with Flask-Caching**: Caching is essential for reducing the load on your database and speeding up responses. **Flask-Caching** can be used to store

frequently accessed data in memory, reducing the number of times the server has to query the database.
Example:
bash
CopyEdit

```
pip install flask-caching
```

python
CopyEdit

```python
from flask import Flask
from flask_caching import Cache

app = Flask(__name__)
app.config['CACHE_TYPE'] = 'simple'
cache = Cache(app)

@app.route('/data')
@cache.cached(timeout=50)
def get_data():
    return {"message": "This is cached data"}
```

2. **Horizontal Scaling with Load Balancers**: Horizontal scaling involves adding more servers or containers to handle increased traffic. You can distribute incoming traffic across multiple instances of your Flask application using a **load balancer**. This prevents any single server from being overwhelmed by requests.

Microservices Architecture: For large enterprise systems, it's often beneficial to break the application into smaller, independently deployable services (microservices). Flask is an excellent choice for creating microservices due to its modularity. Each microservice can focus on a specific business function (e.g., user authentication, payment processing) and communicate with other services via REST APIs.
Example structure:
bash
CopyEdit

```
/user-service
/order-service
/payment-service
```

1. **Database Optimization**: As your application scales, the database becomes a critical bottleneck. Use **SQLAlchemy** with **connection pooling** or consider **NoSQL databases** like **MongoDB** if your data needs are less structured. Employ **database sharding** or **replication** to spread the load across multiple database instances.

Asynchronous Processing with Celery: Flask is synchronous by default, which means it processes one request at a time per worker. For long-running tasks (e.g., sending emails, processing large datasets), it's better to handle these asynchronously. **Celery** integrates seamlessly with Flask to offload tasks to background workers, allowing Flask to remain responsive to incoming API requests.

Example setup with Celery:

bash

CopyEdit

```
pip install celery
```

python

CopyEdit

```
from celery import Celery

app = Flask(__name__)
app.config['CELERY_BROKER_URL'] = 'redis://localhost:6379/0'
celery = Celery(app.name, broker=app.config['CELERY_BROKER_URL'])

@celery.task
def long_task():
    # Simulate a long task
    return 'Task Complete'

@app.route('/start-task')
def start_task():
    long_task.apply_async()
    return "Task started"
```

2. API Rate Limiting: To prevent abuse and ensure fair usage of your resources, implement **rate limiting** for your Flask API. This ensures that clients can only make a specified number of requests in a given period. **Flask-Limiter** is an excellent extension for this.

Example:
bash
CopyEdit

```
pip install flask-limiter
```

python
CopyEdit

```
from flask import Flask
from flask_limiter import Limiter

app = Flask(__name__)
limiter = Limiter(app)

@app.route('/restricted')
@limiter.limit('5 per minute')
def restricted():
    return "This endpoint is rate-limited."
```

Health Checks and Monitoring: In production environments, it's important to monitor the health of your application. Tools like **Prometheus**, **Grafana**, and **New Relic** can provide real-time performance metrics, while health check endpoints in Flask can help with automatic monitoring.

Example health check endpoint:
python
CopyEdit

```
@app.route('/health')
def health():
    return jsonify({"status": "ok"})
```

12.5 Case Study: Flask for Financial APIs

The financial industry relies heavily on data accuracy, real-time transactions, and security. **Flask** is increasingly being used to build financial APIs that provide users with access to financial data, support real-time transactions, and integrate with third-party financial services. Flask's simplicity, combined with its support for asynchronous processing and integration with secure payment systems, makes it a great choice for building financial applications.

Why Flask for Financial APIs?

1. **Fast Development**: Flask's minimalistic approach allows developers to quickly build and deploy financial APIs, making it an excellent choice for fintech startups or companies that need rapid iteration.
2. **Security**: Flask provides robust support for integrating security features like **JWT** (JSON Web Tokens) and **OAuth2** for secure user authentication and authorization.
3. **Scalability**: Flask's flexibility allows developers to scale their APIs as needed. Whether it's adding endpoints for more financial services or handling increased traffic during market hours, Flask can handle the demands of large-scale financial systems.
4. **Integration with Financial Protocols**: Flask can easily integrate with financial services such as payment gateways (e.g., **Stripe**, **PayPal**), financial data providers (e.g., **Quandl**, **Plaid**), and stock market APIs.

Case Study: Building a Payment Gateway API with Flask

Let's look at a real-world example of using Flask to build a **payment gateway API** that processes online transactions.

Key Features:

- **User Authentication**: Secure login using **OAuth2** or **JWT**.
- **Transaction Management**: Support for initiating, processing, and tracking transactions.
- **Payment Gateway Integration**: Integration with payment providers like **Stripe** or **PayPal** for processing payments.
- **Fraud Detection**: APIs to check transactions for suspicious behavior (e.g., using IP geolocation, device fingerprinting, etc.).
- **Real-time Transaction Updates**: Webhooks or SocketIO for pushing updates to users and administrators when transactions are completed or failed.

Example Code for Payment Gateway Integration with Flask and Stripe:

```python
CopyEdit
import stripe
from flask import Flask, jsonify, request
```

```python
app = Flask(__name__)

stripe.api_key = 'sk_test_4eC39HqLyjWDarjtT1zdp7dc'  # Replace with your Stripe
API key

@app.route('/create-payment-intent', methods=['POST'])
def create_payment():
    try:
        data = request.get_json()
        amount = data['amount']  # Amount in cents

        payment_intent = stripe.PaymentIntent.create(
            amount=amount,
            currency='usd',
            payment_method_types=['card'],
        )

        return jsonify({
            'client_secret': payment_intent.client_secret
        })
    except Exception as e:
        return jsonify(error=str(e)), 400

@app.route('/payment-webhook', methods=['POST'])
def handle_payment_webhook():
    payload = request.get_data(as_text=True)
    sig_header = request.headers.get('Stripe-Signature')
    endpoint_secret = 'whsec_12345'  # Replace with your Stripe webhook secret

    event = None
    try:
        event = stripe.Webhook.construct_event(
            payload, sig_header, endpoint_secret
        )
    except ValueError as e:
        return jsonify({'message': 'Invalid payload'}), 400
    except stripe.error.SignatureVerificationError as e:
        return jsonify({'message': 'Invalid signature'}), 400
```

```python
    if event['type'] == 'payment_intent.succeeded':
        payment_intent = event['data']['object']
        print(f"Payment for {payment_intent['amount_received']} was successful.")

    return jsonify({'status': 'success'}), 200

if __name__ == '__main__':
    app.run(debug=True)
```

In this example:

- **/create-payment-intent** creates a new payment intent using the **Stripe API**, specifying the amount and currency.
- **/payment-webhook** handles webhook notifications from Stripe when a payment is processed, confirming successful or failed transactions.

Case Study: Flask for Financial Data Aggregation

Another example of Flask in the financial world is **financial data aggregation**. Flask can be used to create APIs that pull in financial data from third-party services (e.g., stock prices, exchange rates, market news) and aggregate it into a unified API.

Key Features:

- **Data Aggregation**: Integrating data from different sources like **Alpha Vantage**, **Quandl**, or **Plaid** to provide financial data in one place.
- **Real-Time Stock Data**: Building APIs that provide live stock data, such as prices, historical trends, and forecasts.
- **Investment Analysis**: Providing tools for financial analysis, including portfolio management, risk analysis, and investment recommendations.

Chapter 13: Troubleshooting and Debugging Flask APIs

13.1 Common Flask Issues and How to Solve Them

Flask, as a lightweight and flexible micro-framework, is widely used for building web applications and APIs. However, like any development framework, Flask can present challenges that developers must address during the development and deployment phases. Here, we will cover some of the most common Flask issues and provide solutions to troubleshoot and resolve them effectively.

1. Flask Application Not Running

One of the most common issues developers encounter is that their Flask application does not start or runs incorrectly. This could happen due to various reasons, such as missing dependencies, incorrect configurations, or issues in the code itself.

Potential Causes:

- Incorrect app instantiation: If you miss the proper setup of the app instance, Flask won't know how to start the server.
- Missing or outdated dependencies: Flask may require specific versions of libraries.
- Syntax or runtime errors in the app code.

Solutions:

Check the Flask app instance: Ensure that your Flask app instance is properly instantiated in your application file.
python
CopyEdit
```python
from flask import Flask
app = Flask(__name__)
```

Review dependencies: Make sure that you've installed all required dependencies. Use a requirements.txt file to list the necessary packages.

bash

CopyEdit

```
pip install -r requirements.txt
```

Check for syntax errors: Always check the error messages displayed in the console or browser when Flask starts. These messages will often provide a hint as to what went wrong. You can also enable Flask's debugger for more detailed error output.

python

CopyEdit

```
if __name__ == '__main__':
    app.run(debug=True)
```

2. 404 Not Found Error

A frequent issue when building APIs is receiving a **404 Not Found** error, which means the requested URL path does not exist in your application.

Potential Causes:

- Misconfigured or missing route decorators.
- Incorrect URL or HTTP method used in the client request.

Solutions:

Check Route Decorators: Ensure that you have defined the correct route for the endpoint and specified the correct HTTP methods.

python

CopyEdit

```
@app.route('/myendpoint', methods=['GET'])
def my_endpoint():
    return "Hello, World!"
```

- **Verify the URL Path**: Double-check that the client is sending requests to the correct path and using the proper HTTP method. A common mistake is using a POST request for an endpoint that only accepts GET requests.

Ensure Correct HTTP Method: Flask routes can be restricted to specific HTTP methods. If you define a route for GET, it won't accept POST requests unless explicitly allowed.
python
CopyEdit

```python
@app.route('/submit', methods=['POST'])
def submit_data():
    return "Data submitted!"
```

3. Internal Server Error (500)

The **500 Internal Server Error** is another common issue indicating that something went wrong on the server side, but the server cannot or will not be more specific.

Potential Causes:

- Unhandled exceptions in your code.
- Missing or incorrect configurations, especially when connecting to external services or databases.
- Resource exhaustion, like memory limits being exceeded.

Solutions:

Enable Flask Debugging: The Flask debugging mode provides more detailed error information, including the stack trace, making it easier to pinpoint the issue.
python
CopyEdit

```python
app.run(debug=True)
```

Log Errors: Use Flask's built-in logging functionality to capture error messages and gain insights into the problem.

python
CopyEdit

```
import logging
logging.basicConfig(level=logging.DEBUG)
```

- **Check Server Logs**: If Flask is deployed in production, examine the server logs for any exceptions or error messages that can point to the underlying issue.

4. CORS Issues (Cross-Origin Resource Sharing)

When your Flask API is being consumed by a client from a different domain (e.g., a frontend hosted on a different server), you may encounter **CORS (Cross-Origin Resource Sharing)** issues.

Potential Causes:

- The server does not allow cross-origin requests from certain domains or the client domain is not specified in the allowed list.

Solutions:

Use Flask-CORS: Flask-CORS is a popular extension that makes it easy to handle CORS issues.

bash
CopyEdit

```
pip install flask-cors
```

In your Flask app:

python
CopyEdit

```
from flask_cors import CORS
app = Flask(__name__)
CORS(app)
```

222

Configure Allowed Origins: You can specify the allowed origins more specifically:
python
CopyEdit
CORS(app, origins=["https://myfrontend.com"])

5. Template Rendering Issues

Another common issue in Flask is **template rendering** problems, such as templates not loading correctly, or variable data not being passed properly.

Potential Causes:

- The template file does not exist at the specified location.
- Variables or data passed to the template are incorrect or undefined.

Solutions:

Verify Template File Location: Ensure that the templates are in the correct directory (usually a folder named templates) and that they are being loaded correctly.
python
CopyEdit
return render_template('index.html', name='John')

Check Passed Variables: Make sure the data being passed to the template is correctly formatted.
html
CopyEdit
<h1>Hello, {{ name }}</h1>

Use url_for for Static Files: If static files (e.g., CSS, JavaScript) aren't loading, use Flask's url_for to generate the correct URL for static files.
html
CopyEdit
<link rel="stylesheet" href="{{ url_for('static', filename='styles.css') }}">

223

13.2 Troubleshooting Database Connection Issues

Database connectivity issues are one of the most common problems when developing Flask APIs. Whether you're using **SQLAlchemy**, **MongoDB**, or any other database system, connectivity issues can arise due to configuration errors, authentication failures, or network problems.

1. Database Connection Refused

One of the most common errors you might encounter is when your Flask application fails to connect to the database, resulting in a "connection refused" error.

Potential Causes:

- The database service is not running or is unreachable.
- Incorrect database URI or credentials in the application configuration.

Solutions:

Verify Database Status: Ensure that the database service is running. For example, for PostgreSQL, use:

```bash
CopyEdit
sudo service postgresql status
```

Check Database URI: Make sure the database URI in your Flask application configuration is correct. It should follow the correct format for your database (e.g., PostgreSQL, MySQL).

```python
CopyEdit
app.config['SQLALCHEMY_DATABASE_URI'] =
'postgresql://user:password@localhost/mydatabase'
```

- **Firewall or Network Issues**: If the database is hosted remotely, ensure there are no firewall or network issues preventing the connection.

- **Database Logs**: If you're using a managed database service (like Amazon RDS or Azure Database), check the service logs for any connection or authentication issues.

2. SQLAlchemy Session Issues

When using **SQLAlchemy**, you may encounter issues related to the session, such as connection pooling problems or transactions not being committed.

Potential Causes:

- Misconfigured session settings or connection pooling.
- Transactions not being committed or rolled back.

Solutions:

Use Session Commit: Ensure that each transaction is committed to the database.
python
CopyEdit
db.session.commit()

- **Check Session Expiry**: SQLAlchemy sessions may expire if they are left open too long. Ensure that you're closing the session properly.
  python
  CopyEdit
  db.session.remove()

- **Configure Connection Pooling**: If you are dealing with high traffic, configure **connection pooling** to optimize database connections.
  python
  CopyEdit
  app.config['SQLALCHEMY_POOL_SIZE'] = 10

app.config['SQLALCHEMY_POOL_RECYCLE'] = 300

3. Database Migration Issues

Flask often uses **Flask-Migrate** with **Alembic** to handle database migrations. Migration issues can arise, especially if the database schema gets out of sync with your models.

Potential Causes:

225

- Migration files are missing or out of sync.
- Incorrect or missing database schema updates.

Solutions:

Check Migration Status: Run the following commands to check the migration status:
bash
CopyEdit
```
flask db current
flask db migrate
flask db upgrade
```

- **Resolve Conflicts**: If you encounter conflicts with migrations, check for any missing or conflicting migrations and resolve them manually.

4. Database Authentication Issues

Authentication problems with the database can prevent Flask from accessing data, leading to errors like "access denied."

Potential Causes:

- Incorrect username or password.
- Insufficient privileges for the database user.

Solutions:

Verify Database Credentials: Ensure that the database user credentials are correct and that the user has the required permissions.
bash
CopyEdit
```
GRANT ALL PRIVILEGES ON DATABASE mydatabase TO myuser;
```
- **Check Database Access Logs**: Many databases, such as PostgreSQL and MySQL, have access logs that can provide additional insights into authentication issues.

13.3 Debugging Authentication Problems

Authentication is a critical part of any API, and it's common for developers to encounter issues with user authentication, especially when dealing with **JWT** (JSON Web Tokens), **OAuth**, or custom authentication mechanisms. Addressing authentication problems promptly is essential to maintaining the security and functionality of your Flask API.

1. Invalid JWT Tokens

If you're using JWT-based authentication in your Flask API, users may encounter issues with invalid or expired tokens.

Potential Causes:

- The token is expired or malformed.
- Incorrect token decoding or verification.

Solutions:

Verify Token Expiry: Ensure that JWT tokens are not expired. You can include an expiration time (exp) when generating the token and check it during validation.
Example:
python
CopyEdit

```
from datetime import timedelta
access_token = create_access_token(identity=user_id,
expires_delta=timedelta(hours=1))
```

- **Decode the Token Correctly**: If you're manually decoding the token, ensure you're using the correct secret key and that the token format is correct.
  Example:
  python
  CopyEdit

  ```
  from flask_jwt_extended import decode_token
  ```

```
token_data = decode_token(jwt_token)
```

2. OAuth Authentication Issues

OAuth authentication can present challenges, such as issues with token exchange, misconfigured client secrets, or improper redirect URIs.

Potential Causes:

- Invalid client ID or secret.
- Incorrect redirect URI during OAuth flow.

Solutions:

- **Check Client Configuration**: Verify that the OAuth client ID, client secret, and redirect URI are correctly configured in both the Flask app and the OAuth provider (e.g., Google, GitHub).
- **Inspect OAuth Flow**: Ensure that the OAuth flow is correctly implemented, from authorization to token exchange. Many OAuth providers offer detailed logs that can help diagnose issues.

3. User Session Issues

In Flask, user sessions can be managed using **Flask-Login** or custom session management techniques. Problems with sessions may result in users not staying logged in or being redirected to the login page.

Potential Causes:

- Missing session cookies or incorrect session handling.
- The session is not being persisted correctly.

Solutions:

Set SESSION_COOKIE_SECURE: Ensure that session cookies are set correctly, especially when deploying in a production environment. Use secure cookies for production:

python
CopyEdit

```python
app.config['SESSION_COOKIE_SECURE'] = True
```

- **Check Session Expiry**: Ensure that session expiration timeouts are set correctly, and that users aren't logged out prematurely.

4. Insufficient User Permissions

If users are able to authenticate but cannot access certain resources, it may be a problem with insufficient user roles or permissions.

Potential Causes:

- Missing or incorrect role-based access control (RBAC) setup.
- Authentication mechanisms not properly mapping users to their roles.

Solutions:

Define RBAC: If using role-based access control (RBAC), ensure that roles and permissions are defined and mapped correctly in your application.
Example:
python
CopyEdit

```
@app.route('/admin')
@login_required
@roles_required('admin')
def admin():
    return "Welcome Admin!"
```

Authentication issues are common but can be resolved with systematic debugging. Whether it's JWT validation errors, OAuth misconfigurations, session problems, or permission-related issues, Flask provides the flexibility to implement robust authentication mechanisms. By reviewing token expiration, OAuth flows, session management, and user permissions, you can quickly identify and solve authentication problems in your Flask API.

13.4 Resolving Performance Bottlenecks

As Flask APIs scale and handle more traffic, performance bottlenecks can become a significant concern. Identifying and resolving these bottlenecks is crucial to ensure that your API can handle a growing number of requests efficiently without compromising user experience. This section focuses on how to identify common performance bottlenecks in Flask applications and how to resolve them effectively.

1. Identifying Performance Bottlenecks

To resolve performance issues, you first need to identify where the bottlenecks are occurring. Common areas to check include:

- **Database Queries**: Database calls are often the most significant bottleneck in web applications, especially when using an ORM like SQLAlchemy. Slow or inefficient database queries can drastically reduce performance.
- **File I/O**: Reading from and writing to files can be slow, especially when dealing with large files or making multiple disk I/O operations.
- **Network Latency**: If your Flask API interacts with third-party APIs or external services, network latency can be a bottleneck.
- **Complex Business Logic**: Performing heavy computations or running complex algorithms during each request can slow down your application.
- **Concurrency Issues**: Flask is synchronous by default, which means it processes one request at a time per worker. If your application handles many simultaneous requests, this could be a bottleneck.

2. Resolving Database Performance Bottlenecks

- **Optimize Queries**: Always use efficient SQL queries, avoid SELECT *, and limit the number of rows fetched from the database. Use **indexing** for frequently queried fields and **join optimization** for related tables.

Use Connection Pooling: In Flask, you can use **SQLAlchemy's connection pooling** to reuse database connections, which reduces overhead and improves performance, especially under high load.
python
CopyEdit
```
app.config['SQLALCHEMY_POOL_SIZE'] = 10

app.config['SQLALCHEMY_POOL_RECYCLE'] = 300
```

- **Implement Pagination**: For endpoints that return large datasets (e.g., product lists), use pagination to return smaller chunks of data.
python

```
@app.route('/items')

def get_items():

    page = request.args.get('page', 1, type=int)

    per_page = request.args.get('per_page', 10, type=int)

    items = Item.query.paginate(page, per_page, False)

    return jsonify([item.name for item in items.items])
```

- **Caching**: Cache database query results for data that doesn't change frequently (e.g., product catalogs). **Flask-Caching** can store data in memory (using Redis or Memcached) to avoid repeated database calls.
  python
  CopyEdit

```
from flask_caching import Cache

cache = Cache(app)


@app.route('/product/<id>')

@cache.cached(timeout=60)

def get_product(id):

    product = Product.query.get(id)

    return jsonify(product)
```

3. Optimizing File I/O Performance

If your Flask API deals with file uploads or reads large files, this can cause significant performance problems, especially when the files are stored locally.

- **Asynchronous File Uploads**: Use **Celery** or **RQ** to offload file uploads to background workers, allowing Flask to continue processing other requests while files are being uploaded or processed.
- **Efficient File Storage**: Consider using cloud storage services like **Amazon S3** or **Google Cloud Storage** instead of local disk storage, as these services are optimized for large-scale file storage and retrieval.

4. Handling Network Latency

- **Asynchronous Communication**: If your Flask API depends on external services (e.g., payment gateways, third-party APIs), consider using asynchronous communication to prevent blocking the Flask worker while waiting for a response from external services. You can use **Celery** for background tasks or leverage **asyncio** with **Quart**, an asynchronous Flask-compatible framework.
- **Caching External API Responses**: Cache responses from external APIs if they do not change frequently, reducing the number of requests to those services and lowering network latency.

5. Optimizing Business Logic

Profiling and Optimization: Use Python's built-in **cProfile** module to profile your application and identify the functions that consume the most time. Once identified, you can optimize the code or offload heavy computations to background tasks.
Example:
bash
CopyEdit

```
python -m cProfile -s time myapp.py
```

- **Avoiding Synchronous Heavy Computation**: If a route performs heavy computations, move these operations to background tasks using **Celery** or another task queue.

6. Handling Concurrency with Flask

Use Multiple Workers: Flask is single-threaded by default, which means it processes requests one at a time. To handle multiple requests simultaneously, deploy Flask with **multiple worker processes** using a production server like **Gunicorn**:
bash

```
gunicorn -w 4 myapp:app
```

- **Switch to Asynchronous Frameworks**: If your API requires high concurrency (e.g., real-time features like chat or notifications), consider using asynchronous frameworks like **FastAPI** or **Quart**, which allow you to handle many requests concurrently.

13.5 Debugging Flask in Production: Best Practices

Debugging in production is challenging but necessary to ensure the health of your Flask API. In a production environment, you need to carefully manage sensitive information, avoid disruptions, and ensure that debugging efforts don't interfere with the user experience.

1. Enable Logging in Production

Logging is critical for tracking errors, understanding how users interact with your API, and identifying performance issues in production. Flask provides built-in logging features, but in a production environment, you should configure robust logging practices.

Solutions:

Use a Logging Framework: Use Python's built-in **logging** module to capture errors and application activity in production. Set up logging to capture critical information while avoiding unnecessary logs that could overwhelm the system.
python
CopyEdit
```python
import logging

from logging.handlers import RotatingFileHandler


handler = RotatingFileHandler('app.log', maxBytes=10000, backupCount=3)

handler.setLevel(logging.INFO)

app.logger.addHandler(handler)
```
233

- **Send Logs to a Centralized System**: For large-scale applications, sending logs to a centralized system like **Splunk**, **Papertrail**, or **Loggly** allows you to aggregate logs, search for specific errors, and monitor your application in real time.

2. Handling Errors Gracefully

In production, errors should be handled gracefully to avoid showing sensitive information to the user while providing useful error responses.

Solutions:

Custom Error Pages: Flask allows you to customize error pages for common HTTP errors like 404 and 500.
python
CopyEdit
```
@app.errorhandler(404)

def page_not_found(error):

    return render_template('404.html'), 404


@app.errorhandler(500)

def internal_server_error(error):

    return render_template('500.html'), 500
```

- **Avoid Exposing Stack Traces**: Do not expose detailed error messages or stack traces to end users in production. Ensure that Flask's **debug mode** is off in production environments.

3. Monitor Application Health

Monitoring application health is crucial in a production environment. You can set up health check endpoints to monitor the status of your application and ensure it's running as expected.

Solutions:

Health Check Endpoint: Create a simple health check route to return a status message, which can be monitored by tools like **Prometheus** or **New Relic**.
python
CopyEdit

```
@app.route('/health')

def health():

    return jsonify({'status': 'ok'})
```

- **Third-Party Monitoring Tools**: Use services like **New Relic**, **Datadog**, or **Prometheus** to monitor the application's performance and detect anomalies or errors in real time.

4. Use Debugging Tools for Production

While **debug mode** should always be turned off in production, you can still use production-level debugging tools to investigate issues.

Solutions:

Sentry: Sentry is a popular error tracking tool that captures and aggregates errors in your Flask app. It provides stack traces and the context needed to fix issues in real time.
bash
CopyEdit

```
pip install sentry-sdk
```

Example setup in Flask:
python
CopyEdit

```
import sentry_sdk

from sentry_sdk.integrations.flask import FlaskIntegration


sentry_sdk.init(
```

```
dsn="your_sentry_dsn",

integrations=[FlaskIntegration()]

}
```

- **Flask-DebugToolbar**: Flask-DebugToolbar provides a rich interface for debugging in development, but it should never be used in production. However, in production environments, you can configure it to provide limited, non-sensitive debug information.

5. Rollback or Hotfix Strategies

In production, it's critical to have a strategy in place to roll back to a stable version or quickly deploy a hotfix if a bug is found.

Solutions:

- **Version Control and CI/CD**: Use **Git** or another version control system to manage code versions. Set up **CI/CD pipelines** for easy rollbacks and fast deployment of hotfixes.
- **Blue-Green Deployment**: Blue-green deployment strategies allow you to maintain two production environments (Blue and Green) and switch between them in case of failures, providing zero-downtime updates.

13.6 Advanced Flask Debugging Tools and Techniques

Advanced debugging tools and techniques are essential for maintaining the stability and performance of your Flask API in a production environment. While Flask provides some basic debugging tools out of the box, there are several additional tools and strategies that can make troubleshooting and debugging much more effective.

1. Flask-DebugToolbar

Flask-DebugToolbar is an extension that provides a toolbar for inspecting Flask applications. It can display useful information about the request, response, template rendering, database queries, and more. It is a great tool for development but should not be used in production.

Key Features:

- Displays the request context and response time.
- Shows detailed SQLAlchemy query statistics.
- Tracks template rendering times.

Installation:

bash

CopyEdit

pip install flask-debugtoolbar

Example:

python

CopyEdit

from flask_debugtoolbar import DebugToolbarExtension

app = Flask(__name__)

app.config['SECRET_KEY'] = 'supersecretkey'

app.config['DEBUG_TB_INTERCEPT_REDIRECTS'] = False

toolbar = DebugToolbarExtension(app)

2. PyCharm or Visual Studio Code Debugger

For more advanced debugging, using an Integrated Development Environment (IDE) like **PyCharm** or **Visual Studio Code** provides powerful debugging features. These

IDEs allow you to set breakpoints, inspect variable values, step through code, and evaluate expressions without manually adding print() statements.

- **PyCharm** provides an interactive Python console, inline debugging, and can even visualize data structures in real time.
- **Visual Studio Code** supports Python debugging with extensions and offers features like live reload, breakpoints, and variable inspection.

3. Profiling Flask Applications with cProfile

When it comes to performance profiling, **cProfile** is a powerful tool for identifying which parts of your code are consuming the most time.

Installation: cProfile is included in the Python standard library, so you don't need to install anything.

Example Usage:

bash

CopyEdit

```
python -m cProfile -s time app.py
```

This will provide you with detailed statistics about the time spent on each function call, which you can use to optimize your application's performance.

4. Remote Debugging with debugpy

For production environments, where direct access to the server is not always possible, **debugpy** provides a solution for remote debugging. It allows you to debug your Flask application remotely, making it easier to find issues without having direct access to the server's console.

Installation:

bash

CopyEdit

```
pip install debugpy
```

Example Usage:

python

CopyEdit

```
import debugpy


debugpy.listen(("0.0.0.0", 5678))
print("Waiting for debugger to attach...")
debugpy.wait_for_client()


# Your Flask app code here
```

5. Flask-SQLAlchemy Debugging

Flask-SQLAlchemy comes with built-in debugging tools to log SQL queries, which can be invaluable for troubleshooting database-related issues. You can enable query logging to inspect what's going wrong with your queries.

python

CopyEdit

```
app.config['SQLALCHEMY_ECHO'] = True  # Log SQL queries
```

This will print all SQL queries executed by SQLAlchemy to the console, which is helpful for identifying inefficient queries or incorrect database operations.

Advanced debugging tools like **Flask-DebugToolbar**, **PyCharm**, **cProfile**, and **debugpy** make it easier to troubleshoot Flask applications both in development and production environments. Using these tools in conjunction with effective logging,

239

profiling, and error tracking strategies will significantly improve your ability to detect, debug, and resolve issues in your Flask API

Chapter 14: Flask and Frontend Integration

14.1 Integrating Flask APIs with ReactJS

Flask, as a backend framework, is often paired with modern frontend libraries and frameworks like **ReactJS** to create dynamic, full-stack web applications. ReactJS is a powerful JavaScript library for building user interfaces, particularly single-page applications (SPAs) that update dynamically without reloading the entire page. Integrating Flask with React allows you to leverage Flask's simplicity for building RESTful APIs and React's efficiency for building interactive, user-centric interfaces.

Setting Up the Project

To integrate Flask with ReactJS, you typically follow a **frontend-backend separation** approach where Flask serves as the API provider, and React handles the frontend UI. This separation allows Flask to manage business logic, database connections, and user authentication, while React handles rendering and state management.

Steps to Integrate Flask with ReactJS:

1. **Set Up Flask API**: First, create a simple Flask API that will serve as the backend for your React frontend.
   Example Flask Backend:
   python
   CopyEdit
   ```python
   from flask import Flask, jsonify, request

   app = Flask(__name__)

   @app.route('/api/data', methods=['GET'])
   def get_data():
       return jsonify({"message": "Hello from Flask!"})

   if __name__ == "__main__":
       app.run(debug=True)
   ```

   This Flask application has an API endpoint (/api/data) that returns a JSON object when accessed via a GET request.

241

2. **Create React Application**: Use **Create React App** (CRA) to quickly set up a
   React project.
   bash
   CopyEdit

```
npx create-react-app my-react-app
cd my-react-app
npm start
```

3. **Install Axios for HTTP Requests**: To make HTTP requests from React to the
   Flask backend, use a library like **Axios**, which is simple to use and works well
   with APIs.
   bash
   CopyEdit

```
npm install axios
```

4. **Create React Component to Fetch Data**: Now, you can create a React
   component that makes a GET request to the Flask API and displays the result.
   Example React Component:
   javascript
   CopyEdit

```
import React, { useEffect, useState } from 'react';
import axios from 'axios';

function App() {
  const [data, setData] = useState(null);

  useEffect(() => {
    axios.get('http://localhost:5000/api/data')
      .then(response => {
        setData(response.data.message);
      })
      .catch(error => {
        console.error('Error fetching data:', error);
      });
  }, []);
```

```
return (
  <div className="App">
    <h1>{data ? data : "Loading..."}</h1>
  </div>
);
}

export default App;
```

> In this example:
> - The useEffect hook is used to fetch data from the Flask API when the component mounts.
> - **Axios** is used to send the GET request to the Flask API and handle the response.

CORS Configuration: To allow React (running on a different port) to communicate with Flask, you need to enable **CORS (Cross-Origin Resource Sharing)** on the Flask backend. This can be done using the flask-cors extension.
bash
CopyEdit
pip install flask-cors
In your Flask app, enable CORS:
python
CopyEdit
from flask_cors import CORS

app = Flask(__name__)
CORS(app) # Enable CORS for all routes

14.2 Using Flask with Vue.js for SPA (Single Page Applications)

Vue.js is another modern JavaScript framework used for building interactive UIs and SPAs. Similar to React, Vue.js allows you to build highly dynamic, component-based applications. When integrated with Flask, Vue.js handles the frontend logic and user interface, while Flask manages the backend functionality, including data processing, authentication, and database management.

243

Setting Up the Project

Integrating Flask with Vue.js is similar to integrating Flask with React. The primary difference is in the frontend framework used. Below is a guide to setting up a Flask and Vue.js application for building an SPA.

Set Up Flask API: Create a simple Flask API to provide data for the Vue.js frontend.
Example Flask Backend:
python
CopyEdit
```python
from flask import Flask, jsonify

app = Flask(__name__)

@app.route('/api/data', methods=['GET'])
def get_data():
    return jsonify({"message": "Hello from Flask!"})

if __name__ == "__main__":
    app.run(debug=True)
```

Create Vue.js Application: Use Vue CLI to create a new Vue.js project.
bash
CopyEdit
```bash
npm install -g @vue/cli
vue create my-vue-app
cd my-vue-app
npm run serve
```

Install Axios for HTTP Requests: To interact with the Flask API, install **Axios** in your Vue.js project.
bash
CopyEdit
```bash
npm install axios
```

244

Create a Vue Component to Fetch Data: Use **Axios** to send a GET request to the Flask API and display the data in a Vue component.

Example Vue Component:

vue

CopyEdit

```
<template>
 <div>
  <h1>{{ message }}</h1>
 </div>
</template>

<script>
import axios from 'axios';

export default {
 data() {
  return {
   message: 'Loading...'
  };
 },
 created() {
  axios.get('http://localhost:5000/api/data')
   .then(response => {
    this.message = response.data.message;
   })
   .catch(error => {
    console.error('Error fetching data:', error);
   });
 }
};
</script>
```

In this example:
- The created lifecycle hook fetches data from the Flask API as soon as the component is created.
- The fetched message is displayed in an <h1> tag.

245

CORS Configuration: As with React, enable **CORS** on the Flask server to allow requests from a different port (Vue.js frontend).

bash
CopyEdit

```
pip install flask-cors
```

Enable CORS in your Flask application:

python
CopyEdit

```
from flask_cors import CORS

app = Flask(__name__)
CORS(app)  # Allow all origins by default
```

14.3 Handling Form Data from Frontend to Flask Backend

Handling form data is a common requirement in web applications. Whether it's handling user registration, contact forms, or search forms, Flask provides tools to easily accept and process data from the frontend. In this section, we'll cover how to handle form data from the frontend (whether via regular HTML forms or JavaScript-based forms) and process it using Flask.

1. Sending Form Data with HTML Forms

Flask provides an easy way to accept data from HTML forms. The data sent by the form can be accessed via request.form, which contains key-value pairs for the form fields.

Example HTML Form:

html
CopyEdit

```
<form action="/submit" method="POST">
  <input type="text" name="username" placeholder="Enter your username">
  <input type="password" name="password" placeholder="Enter your password">
  <button type="submit">Submit</button>
</form>
```

In the above example, when the form is submitted, it sends the data to the /submit route using the POST method.

Example Flask Backend:

python
CopyEdit
```python
from flask import Flask, request

app = Flask(__name__)

@app.route('/submit', methods=['POST'])
def submit_form():
    username = request.form['username']
    password = request.form['password']
    return f'Username: {username}, Password: {password}'

if __name__ == '__main__':
    app.run(debug=True)
```

In this example:

- The request.form dictionary is used to retrieve the form data (username and password).
- Flask then processes this data and returns a response containing the received data.

2. Sending Form Data with JavaScript (AJAX Requests)

In modern applications, it's common to submit form data without reloading the page, using **AJAX** requests. You can send data from the frontend to Flask using JavaScript and **Axios** or the native fetch API.

Example HTML Form:

html
CopyEdit
```html
<form id="myForm">
  <input type="text" id="username" placeholder="Enter your username">
```

247

```html
<input type="password" id="password" placeholder="Enter your password">
<button type="submit">Submit</button>
</form>
```

JavaScript (AJAX) Submission:

javascript
CopyEdit

```javascript
document.getElementById('myForm').addEventListener('submit', function(e) {
  e.preventDefault();

  let username = document.getElementById('username').value;
  let password = document.getElementById('password').value;

  axios.post('http://localhost:5000/submit', {
    username: username,
    password: password
  })
  .then(response => {
    console.log('Data received:', response.data);
  })
  .catch(error => {
    console.error('Error submitting form:', error);
  });
});
```

Example Flask Backend:

python
CopyEdit

```python
from flask import Flask, request, jsonify

app = Flask(__name__)

@app.route('/submit', methods=['POST'])
def submit_form():
    username = request.json['username']
```

248

```
password = request.json['password']
return jsonify(message=f'Username: {username}, Password: {password}')

if __name__ == '__main__':
    app.run(debug=True)
```

In this example:

- The form data is collected using JavaScript and sent via a POST request to the Flask backend using **Axios**.
- The Flask backend receives the data via request.json (since the data is sent as JSON).

3. Handling File Uploads

Flask also supports handling file uploads, such as profile images or documents. To handle file uploads, you use request.files.

Example HTML File Upload Form:

html
CopyEdit
```html
<form action="/upload" method="POST" enctype="multipart/form-data">
  <input type="file" name="file">
  <button type="submit">Upload</button>
</form>
```

Example Flask Backend for File Upload:

python
CopyEdit
```python
from flask import Flask, request

app = Flask(__name__)

@app.route('/upload', methods=['POST'])
def upload_file():
    file = request.files['file']
```
249

```
file.save(f'./uploads/{file.filename}')
return f'File uploaded: {file.filename}'

if __name__ == '__main__':
    app.run(debug=True)
```

In this example:

- The request.files object is used to access the uploaded file.
- The file is saved to the server's uploads directory.

14.4 Building a Full-Stack Application with Flask and Angular

Angular is a popular framework for building dynamic, client-side web applications, and it can be seamlessly integrated with Flask to create full-stack web applications. Flask will handle the backend logic, business rules, and database interactions, while Angular will manage the frontend, providing an interactive and dynamic user interface.

Setting Up the Project

In a full-stack Flask-Angular application, Flask serves as a RESTful API provider, and Angular handles the frontend and user interactions. The following sections explain how to set up the basic infrastructure for such an application.

Create the Flask Backend: Start by setting up a Flask API to handle requests from the Angular frontend. The Flask API will manage business logic, authentication, and database connections.

Example Flask Backend:
python
CopyEdit
```
from flask import Flask, jsonify, request

from flask_sqlalchemy import SQLAlchemy


app = Flask(__name__)
```

```python
app.config['SQLALCHEMY_DATABASE_URI'] = 'sqlite:///users.db'

db = SQLAlchemy(app)


class User(db.Model):

    id = db.Column(db.Integer, primary_key=True)

    username = db.Column(db.String(100), nullable=False)


@app.route('/api/users', methods=['GET'])

def get_users():

    users = User.query.all()

    return jsonify([{'id': user.id, 'username': user.username} for user in users])


if __name__ == '__main__':

    db.create_all()

    app.run(debug=True)
```

In this simple example:
- The /api/users endpoint returns a list of users from the database in JSON format.
- The application uses SQLAlchemy to interact with a SQLite database for storing user information.

Create the Angular Frontend: Now, set up the Angular frontend to interact with the Flask API. You can use the Angular CLI to generate a new Angular application.
bash
CopyEdit
ng new my-angular-app

```
cd my-angular-app
```

```
ng serve
```

Install Axios for HTTP Requests: Angular has built-in HTTP services, but you can also use **Axios** for making HTTP requests to the Flask API. To install Axios, run the following:
bash
CopyEdit
```
npm install axios
```

Create Angular Service to Fetch Data: Angular services are used to manage data fetching and business logic. Create a service to fetch user data from the Flask API.
Example Angular Service (user.service.ts):
typescript
CopyEdit
```
import { Injectable } from '@angular/core';

import axios from 'axios';


@Injectable({

  providedIn: 'root'

})

export class UserService {


  private apiUrl = 'http://localhost:5000/api/users';


  constructor() { }


  getUsers() {
```

```
    return axios.get(this.apiUrl);

  }

}
```

Create Angular Component to Display Data: Now, create a component that will fetch and display the user data from the Flask API.

Example Angular Component (app.component.ts):

typescript
CopyEdit

```
import { Component, OnInit } from '@angular/core';

import { UserService } from './user.service';


@Component({

  selector: 'app-root',

  templateUrl: './app.component.html',

  styleUrls: ['./app.component.css']

})
export class AppComponent implements OnInit {

  users = [];


  constructor(private userService: UserService) {}


  ngOnInit(): void {

    this.userService.getUsers()

      .then(response => {
```

```
    this.users = response.data;

  })

  .catch(error => {

    console.error('Error fetching users:', error);

  });

 }

}
```

Example Angular HTML Template (app.component.html):
html
CopyEdit
```
<h1>Users List</h1>

<ul>

  <li *ngFor="let user of users">

    {{ user.username }}

  </li>

</ul>
```

Enable CORS in Flask: Since Angular and Flask will be running on different ports, you need to enable **CORS** (Cross-Origin Resource Sharing) on the Flask server to allow requests from the Angular frontend.
Flask CORS Configuration:
bash
CopyEdit
```
pip install flask-cors
```

In your Flask app:
python

254

CopyEdit

```
from flask_cors import CORS

app = Flask(__name__)

CORS(app)  # Enable CORS for all routes
```

Running the Full-Stack Application

Run the Flask application:
bash
CopyEdit

```
python app.py
```

- Run the Angular application:
  bash
  CopyEdit

  ```
  ng serve
  ```

Your Angular frontend will now communicate with your Flask backend, fetching user data from the /api/users endpoint and displaying it dynamically on the webpage.

14.5 Authentication: Flask API + Frontend Integration Best Practices

Integrating user authentication between Flask APIs and frontend applications (React, Angular, Vue.js, etc.) requires careful attention to security, session management, and data validation. Properly handling authentication ensures that only authorized users can access sensitive resources, and it enhances the user experience by providing secure access to various parts of the application.

1. Choosing the Right Authentication Method

There are several authentication methods you can use when integrating Flask with a frontend application. The most common methods include **Token-Based Authentication** (using JWT) and **Session-Based Authentication**.

- **Token-Based Authentication (JWT)**: JSON Web Tokens (JWT) are widely used for stateless authentication. With JWT, the server issues a token upon successful login, which is then used by the client to authenticate subsequent requests.
- **Session-Based Authentication**: This method relies on server-side session storage. When a user logs in, the server creates a session and sends a session ID to the client, which is stored in a cookie. For each subsequent request, the session ID is sent to the server to authenticate the user.

2. Using JWT for Authentication

JWT is ideal for single-page applications (SPA) and APIs because it allows stateless authentication, which is particularly useful for scaling and distributed systems.

Backend (Flask API): In the Flask backend, you'll need to use the **Flask-JWT-Extended** extension to manage JWT-based authentication.
Installation:
bash
CopyEdit
```
pip install flask-jwt-extended
```

Example Flask Setup:
python
CopyEdit
```
from flask import Flask, request, jsonify

from flask_jwt_extended import JWTManager, create_access_token, jwt_required


app = Flask(__name__)

app.config['JWT_SECRET_KEY'] = 'your_jwt_secret_key'

jwt = JWTManager(app)


@app.route('/login', methods=['POST'])

def login():
```

256

```python
    username = request.json.get('username')

    password = request.json.get('password')


    if username == 'user' and password == 'password':  # Dummy check

        access_token = create_access_token(identity=username)

        return jsonify(access_token=access_token), 200


    return jsonify(message="Invalid credentials"), 401


@app.route('/protected', methods=['GET'])

@jwt_required()

def protected():

    return jsonify(message="You have access to this protected route"), 200


if __name__ == '__main__':

    app.run(debug=True)
```

In this example:

- The /login route generates a JWT token when the user provides valid credentials.
- The /protected route is protected and can only be accessed by a user with a valid JWT token.

Frontend (React or Angular): On the frontend, when a user logs in, the JWT is stored (typically in localStorage or sessionStorage) and sent in the Authorization header for subsequent API requests.

257

Example React Component (Login Form):
javascript
CopyEdit

```javascript
import React, { useState } from 'react';

import axios from 'axios';

function LoginForm() {
  const [username, setUsername] = useState('');

  const [password, setPassword] = useState('');

  const [message, setMessage] = useState('');

  const handleLogin = () => {
    axios.post('http://localhost:5000/login', { username, password })

      .then(response => {

        localStorage.setItem('token', response.data.access_token);  // Store the token

        setMessage('Login successful');

      })

      .catch(error => {

        setMessage('Invalid credentials');

      });
  };

  return (
```

258

```jsx
  <div>

    <input type="text" placeholder="Username" onChange={(e) =>
setUsername(e.target.value)} />

    <input type="password" placeholder="Password" onChange={(e) =>
setPassword(e.target.value)} />

    <button onClick={handleLogin}>Login</button>

    <p>{message}</p>

  </div>

 );

}


export default LoginForm;
```

Example React Component (Accessing Protected Route):
javascript
CopyEdit

```javascript
import React, { useState, useEffect } from 'react';

import axios from 'axios';


function ProtectedRoute() {

 const [message, setMessage] = useState('');


 useEffect(() => {

  const token = localStorage.getItem('token');

  axios.get('http://localhost:5000/protected', {
```

```
    headers: {

      Authorization: `Bearer ${token}`

    }

  })

  .then(response => {

    setMessage(response.data.message);

  })

  .catch(error => {

    setMessage('You do not have access');

  });

}, []);


  return <p>{message}</p>;

}


export default ProtectedRoute;
```

3. Handling Session-Based Authentication

If you prefer session-based authentication, Flask's **Flask-Login** extension can be used to manage user sessions.

Installation:

bash

CopyEdit

pip install flask-login

Example Flask Setup with Flask-Login:

python

CopyEdit

```
from flask import Flask, render_template, redirect, url_for, request

from flask_login import LoginManager, UserMixin, login_user, login_required,
logout_user


app = Flask(__name__)

app.secret_key = 'your_secret_key'

login_manager = LoginManager()

login_manager.init_app(app)


class User(UserMixin):

    def __init__(self, id):

        self.id = id


users = {'user': {'password': 'password'}}  # Example user
```

```python
@login_manager.user_loader
def load_user(user_id):
    return User(user_id)


@app.route('/login', methods=['GET', 'POST'])
def login():
    if request.method == 'POST':
        username = request.form['username']
        password = request.form['password']
        if username in users and users[username]['password'] == password:
            user = User(username)
            login_user(user)
            return redirect(url_for('protected'))
    return render_template('login.html')


@app.route('/protected')
@login_required
def protected():
    return 'This is a protected route!'


if __name__ == '__main__':
    app.run(debug=True)
```
262

In this case, Flask-Login is used to manage user login and session creation. The login_required decorator is used to restrict access to certain routes.

4. Best Practices for Authentication

- **Token Storage**: Always store JWT tokens securely on the frontend (e.g., using localStorage, sessionStorage, or cookies with HttpOnly and Secure flags).
- **Use HTTPS**: Always use HTTPS to protect sensitive data like passwords and tokens from being intercepted.
- **Session Expiry**: Set appropriate expiration times for JWT tokens and use refresh tokens to avoid long-lasting sessions.
- **Cross-Origin Resource Sharing (CORS)**: Ensure that you configure CORS correctly to allow your frontend to make requests to your Flask backend.

Chapter 15: Advanced Flask Projects

15.1 Building a RESTful API for an E-Commerce Platform

Building an e-commerce platform involves creating a RESTful API that allows clients (such as web browsers, mobile applications, and third-party services) to interact with your backend. A well-structured API is essential for handling various e-commerce operations like product management, order processing, customer management, and payment gateway integration. Flask is an ideal choice for building the backend of such platforms due to its simplicity, flexibility, and scalability.

Key Features of an E-Commerce RESTful API:

1. **Product Management**: CRUD operations for products (create, read, update, delete).
2. **User Authentication and Authorization**: Register, login, and manage user profiles.
3. **Shopping Cart**: Add/remove products, view cart, and manage quantities.
4. **Order Management**: Place orders, view order history, and track shipping.
5. **Payment Integration**: Handle payment gateway interactions (e.g., Stripe or PayPal).
6. **Review System**: Allow customers to rate and review products.

Setting Up the E-Commerce API with Flask

Set Up Flask Application and Database: First, set up the basic Flask app and the database using SQLAlchemy. The app will handle product data, user profiles, and orders.

Flask Setup:
bash
CopyEdit
```
pip install flask flask-sqlalchemy flask-marshmallow flask-jwt-extended
```
Example Flask Backend for Products and Users:
python
CopyEdit
```
from flask import Flask, request, jsonify
from flask_sqlalchemy import SQLAlchemy
from flask_marshmallow import Marshmallow
```

```
from flask_jwt_extended import JWTManager, create_access_token, jwt_required
app = Flask(__name__)
app.config['SQLALCHEMY_DATABASE_URI'] = 'sqlite:///ecommerce.db'
app.config['JWT_SECRET_KEY'] = 'supersecretkey'
db = SQLAlchemy(app)
ma = Marshmallow(app)
jwt = JWTManager(app)

# Product Model
class Product(db.Model):
    id = db.Column(db.Integer, primary_key=True)
    name = db.Column(db.String(100))
    price = db.Column(db.Float)

# User Model
class User(db.Model):
    id = db.Column(db.Integer, primary_key=True)
    username = db.Column(db.String(100), unique=True)
    password = db.Column(db.String(100))

@app.route('/products', methods=['GET'])
def get_products():
    products = Product.query.all()
    return jsonify([{'name': p.name, 'price': p.price} for p in products])

@app.route('/register', methods=['POST'])
def register_user():
    username = request.json['username']
    password = request.json['password']
    new_user = User(username=username, password=password)
    db.session.add(new_user)
    db.session.commit()
    return jsonify({'message': 'User created successfully'}), 201

@app.route('/login', methods=['POST'])
def login_user():
    username = request.json['username']
    password = request.json['password']
```

```
user = User.query.filter_by(username=username).first()
if user and user.password == password:
    access_token = create_access_token(identity=username)
    return jsonify(access_token=access_token)
return jsonify({'message': 'Invalid credentials'}), 401

if __name__ == '__main__':
    db.create_all()
    app.run(debug=True)
```

1. **Adding More Features**:
   - **Shopping Cart**: The shopping cart can be managed by a separate model and table, storing items added by users, along with quantities.
   - **Order Management**: Create an Order model that links products to users and stores order status.
   - **Payment Integration**: Integrate with **Stripe** or **PayPal** APIs to handle payments.
2. **Handling User Authentication**: Use **JWT (JSON Web Tokens)** for managing user authentication. After logging in, the user receives a token which they can send with every request for authentication. Protect routes that need authentication using @jwt_required().
3. **Database Schema for Products and Orders**: Define your product and order models to allow CRUD operations. Use SQLAlchemy's Model class to define the relationships.
4. **Testing the API**: Use tools like **Postman** or **Insomnia** to test your API endpoints by sending HTTP requests. For example, test registering a user, adding products, and logging in.

15.2 Building a Social Media API with Flask

A social media platform requires an API that can handle multiple users, posts, comments, likes, and interactions. Flask, with its simplicity and powerful extensions, is a great choice for building a social media backend. In this section, we will outline how to build a basic social media API with Flask, covering essential features like user management, posts, and comments.

Key Features of a Social Media API:

1. **User Authentication**: Register, login, and manage user profiles.
2. **Posts**: Create, read, update, and delete posts.
3. **Comments**: Allow users to comment on posts.
4. **Likes**: Users can like posts.
5. **Followers**: Users can follow/unfollow each other.

Setting Up the Social Media API with Flask

Flask Application and Database Setup: Start by creating a Flask application and setting up the database to store user information, posts, comments, and likes.

1. **Install Dependencies**:

bash

CopyEdit

```
pip install flask flask-sqlalchemy flask-marshmallow flask-jwt-extended
```

Example Flask Setup:

python

CopyEdit

```
from flask import Flask, request, jsonify
from flask_sqlalchemy import SQLAlchemy
from flask_marshmallow import Marshmallow
from flask_jwt_extended import JWTManager, create_access_token, jwt_required

app = Flask(__name__)
app.config['SQLALCHEMY_DATABASE_URI'] = 'sqlite:///social_media.db'
app.config['JWT_SECRET_KEY'] = 'secretkey'
db = SQLAlchemy(app)
ma = Marshmallow(app)
jwt = JWTManager(app)

class User(db.Model):
    id = db.Column(db.Integer, primary_key=True)
    username = db.Column(db.String(100), unique=True)
    password = db.Column(db.String(100))

class Post(db.Model):
    id = db.Column(db.Integer, primary_key=True)
    content = db.Column(db.String(200))
```

```python
    user_id = db.Column(db.Integer, db.ForeignKey('user.id'))
    user = db.relationship('User', backref=db.backref('posts', lazy=True))

@app.route('/register', methods=['POST'])
def register_user():
    username = request.json['username']
    password = request.json['password']
    new_user = User(username=username, password=password)
    db.session.add(new_user)
    db.session.commit()
    return jsonify({'message': 'User created successfully'}), 201

@app.route('/login', methods=['POST'])
def login_user():
    username = request.json['username']
    password = request.json['password']
    user = User.query.filter_by(username=username).first()
    if user and user.password == password:
        access_token = create_access_token(identity=username)
        return jsonify(access_token=access_token)
    return jsonify({'message': 'Invalid credentials'}), 401

@app.route('/post', methods=['POST'])
@jwt_required()
def create_post():
    content = request.json['content']
    user_id = request.json['user_id']
    new_post = Post(content=content, user_id=user_id)
    db.session.add(new_post)
    db.session.commit()
    return jsonify({'message': 'Post created'}), 201

@app.route('/posts', methods=['GET'])
def get_posts():
    posts = Post.query.all()
    return jsonify([{'content': p.content, 'username': p.user.username} for p in posts])

if __name__ == '__main__':
```

```
db.create_all()
app.run(debug=True)
```

2. User Authentication and JWT: Use **JWT** to authenticate users and ensure that only authorized users can access certain routes, such as posting content or updating their profile.

3. Posts and Comments: The Post model stores each post's content and the associated user. You can extend this model by adding a Comment model for users to comment on posts.

4. Database Schema: The User and Post models represent basic entities. You can expand the database schema to support features like likes, followers, and multimedia posts.

5. Testing the API: Use **Postman** or **Insomnia** to test the social media API. Test creating accounts, logging in, making posts, and viewing posts.

15.3 Building a Blog API with Flask and SQLAlchemy

A blog API is another common project that showcases the power of Flask and its integrations with databases like **SQLAlchemy**. A blog API typically allows users to create, read, update, and delete blog posts, along with managing user authentication, comments, and tags. This project can serve as the foundation for more advanced applications, such as content management systems (CMS) or news platforms.

Key Features of a Blog API:

1. **User Authentication**: Secure login and registration for authors and readers.
2. **Blog Posts**: CRUD operations for blog posts.
3. **Comments**: Readers can comment on posts.
4. **Tags**: Posts can be categorized using tags.
5. **Post Categorization**: Admins or authors can categorize posts by topic.

Setting Up the Blog API with Flask and SQLAlchemy

Flask Application Setup: First, set up a basic Flask application with SQLAlchemy for database interaction. The blog API will manage posts, users, and comments.

Install Dependencies:
bash
CopyEdit

```
pip install flask flask-sqlalchemy flask-marshmallow flask-jwt-extended
```

Example Flask Blog API:

python

CopyEdit

```python
from flask import Flask, request, jsonify
from flask_sqlalchemy import SQLAlchemy
from flask_marshmallow import Marshmallow
from flask_jwt_extended import JWTManager, create_access_token, jwt_required

app = Flask(__name__)
app.config['SQLALCHEMY_DATABASE_URI'] = 'sqlite:///blog.db'
app.config['JWT_SECRET_KEY'] = 'your_jwt_secret_key'
db = SQLAlchemy(app)
ma = Marshmallow(app)
jwt = JWTManager(app)

class User(db.Model):
    id = db.Column(db.Integer, primary_key=True)
    username = db.Column(db.String(100), unique=True)
    password = db.Column(db.String(100))

class Post(db.Model):
    id = db.Column(db.Integer, primary_key=True)
    title = db.Column(db.String(100))
    content = db.Column(db.String(1000))
    user_id = db.Column(db.Integer, db.ForeignKey('user.id'))
    user = db.relationship('User', backref=db.backref('posts', lazy=True))

@app.route('/register', methods=['POST'])
def register_user():
    username = request.json['username']
    password = request.json['password']
    new_user = User(username=username, password=password)
    db.session.add(new_user)
    db.session.commit()
    return jsonify({'message': 'User created successfully'}), 201

@app.route('/login', methods=['POST'])
def login_user():
```

```
    username = request.json['username']
    password = request.json['password']
    user = User.query.filter_by(username=username).first()
    if user and user.password == password:
        access_token = create_access_token(identity=username)
        return jsonify(access_token=access_token)
    return jsonify({'message': 'Invalid credentials'}), 401
@app.route('/posts', methods=['POST'])
@jwt_required()
def create_post():
    title = request.json['title']
    content = request.json['content']
    user_id = request.json['user_id']
    new_post = Post(title=title, content=content, user_id=user_id)
    db.session.add(new_post)
    db.session.commit()
    return jsonify({'message': 'Post created successfully'}), 201

@app.route('/posts', methods=['GET'])
def get_posts():
    posts = Post.query.all()
    return jsonify([{'title': p.title, 'content': p.content} for p in posts])

if __name__ == '__main__':
    db.create_all()
    app.run(debug=True)
```

1. **Creating Blog Posts and Comments**: The Post model stores each blog post. You can extend this model by adding a Comment model for users to comment on posts.
2. **Handling User Authentication**: Use **JWT** for handling user login and session management. Ensure that only authenticated users can create or edit posts.
3. **Database Schema**: The Post model holds the content of the blog posts, and the User model tracks users. You can add tags and categories by creating additional models or using many-to-many relationships.
4. **Testing the Blog API**: Use **Postman** to test creating users, logging in, creating blog posts, and viewing them.

Building a blog API with Flask and SQLAlchemy provides an excellent foundation for understanding how to manage content-driven applications. By adding features like authentication, comments, and tags, you can expand this basic API into a full-fledged blogging platform or content management system. Flask's lightweight and flexible nature make it the perfect choice for such projects, allowing for scalability and easy integration with frontend technologies.

15.4 Real-Time Chat Application with Flask and WebSockets

A **real-time chat application** is a common use case for building interactive and dynamic systems where users can send and receive messages instantly. Using Flask combined with **WebSockets** enables bidirectional communication between the client and server, providing a foundation for a real-time messaging system. Flask can manage the backend and user authentication, while WebSockets ensure that communication occurs in real-time.

Key Features of a Real-Time Chat Application:

1. **Real-Time Messaging**: Users can send and receive messages instantly without needing to refresh the page.
2. **User Authentication**: Users must log in to send messages.
3. **Private and Group Chats**: Support for one-on-one and group conversations.
4. **Notifications**: Notify users of new messages or when they are mentioned.
5. **Message History**: Storing past messages so users can view them later.

Setting Up the Project

To build a chat application, we need to integrate **Flask** with **WebSockets** using an extension like **Flask-SocketIO**.

Install Flask-SocketIO: Flask-SocketIO allows Flask to handle WebSocket connections and enables real-time communication.
bash
CopyEdit
```
pip install flask-socketio
```

Setting Up Flask Application: Let's create a basic chat app with Flask and WebSockets.
Example Flask Chat Backend:
python
CopyEdit
```python
from flask import Flask, render_template

from flask_socketio import SocketIO, emit


app = Flask(__name__)

socketio = SocketIO(app)


@app.route('/')

def index():

    return render_template('index.html')


@socketio.on('message')

def handle_message(data):

    print(f"Message received: {data}")

    emit('response', {'message': data}, broadcast=True)


if __name__ == '__main__':

    socketio.run(app, debug=True)
```

In this example:
- We import **SocketIO** and initialize it with the Flask app.

- o The handle_message function listens for incoming messages on the WebSocket connection, and emit sends that message to all connected clients (broadcasting).

Setting Up the Frontend: The frontend will use **JavaScript** to interact with the WebSocket connection. We'll use a simple HTML page with a chat input and display area for messages.

Example HTML (index.html):

html
CopyEdit

```html
<!DOCTYPE html>

<html lang="en">

<head>

  <meta charset="UTF-8">

  <title>Real-Time Chat</title>

  <script src="https://cdnjs.cloudflare.com/ajax/libs/socket.io/4.0.1/socket.io.min.js"></script>

</head>

<body>

  <h1>Real-Time Chat Application</h1>

  <div id="messages"></div>

  <input type="text" id="message" placeholder="Type a message..." />

  <button onclick="sendMessage()">Send</button>


  <script>

    const socket = io.connect('http://localhost:5000');
```

```
socket.on('response', function(data) {

    const messages = document.getElementById('messages');

    messages.innerHTML += `<p>${data.message}</p>`;

});


function sendMessage() {

    const message = document.getElementById('message').value;

    socket.send(message);

    document.getElementById('message').value = '';  // Clear input

}
</script>
</body>
</html>
```

In this frontend:
- The **Socket.IO client** connects to the Flask server.
- When a user sends a message, it triggers the sendMessage function, which sends the message to the server over WebSocket.
- The server broadcasts the message back to all connected clients, and the frontend displays it in real-time.

Running the Application:

Run the Flask app:
bash
CopyEdit
python app.py

- Open multiple browser tabs or windows to simulate multiple users and interact with the chat in real-time.

15.5 Building a Financial Dashboard API with Flask and React

A **financial dashboard** API is designed to fetch, process, and display financial data, such as stock prices, market trends, and user portfolios. Building a **Flask API** for a financial dashboard can handle the backend logic and data management, while **React** serves as the frontend for displaying dynamic charts, financial data, and reports in real-time.

Key Features of a Financial Dashboard:

1. **Market Data**: Display real-time stock prices and financial metrics.
2. **User Portfolio**: Allow users to track their investments and portfolio value.
3. **Interactive Charts**: Visualize financial data using interactive charts and graphs.
4. **User Authentication**: Secure access to the dashboard with user-specific data.

Setting Up the Project

To build this dashboard, Flask will act as the backend API, providing financial data and handling user authentication, while React will manage the frontend display and interactivity.

Set Up Flask Backend: The Flask backend will provide endpoints to fetch financial data, such as stock prices, market trends, and user portfolios.
Install Dependencies:
bash
CopyEdit
```
pip install flask flask-sqlalchemy flask-marshmallow flask-jwt-extended
```

Example Flask Backend:
python
CopyEdit
```
from flask import Flask, request, jsonify

from flask_sqlalchemy import SQLAlchemy

from flask_jwt_extended import JWTManager, create_access_token, jwt_required


app = Flask(__name__)
```

```python
app.config['SQLALCHEMY_DATABASE_URI'] = 'sqlite:///financial_data.db'

app.config['JWT_SECRET_KEY'] = 'secretkey'

db = SQLAlchemy(app)

jwt = JWTManager(app)


class Portfolio(db.Model):
    id = db.Column(db.Integer, primary_key=True)

    stock_name = db.Column(db.String(100))

    quantity = db.Column(db.Integer)

    user_id = db.Column(db.Integer)


@app.route('/login', methods=['POST'])
def login_user():
    username = request.json['username']

    password = request.json['password']

    # Dummy check (use proper auth in production)

    if username == 'user' and password == 'password':

        access_token = create_access_token(identity=username)

        return jsonify(access_token=access_token)

    return jsonify({'message': 'Invalid credentials'}), 401


@app.route('/portfolio', methods=['GET'])
```

277

```python
@jwt_required()
def get_portfolio():
    portfolio = Portfolio.query.all()
    return jsonify([{'stock_name': p.stock_name, 'quantity': p.quantity} for p in portfolio])


if __name__ == '__main__':
    db.create_all()
    app.run(debug=True)
```

- This API provides a /portfolio endpoint that retrieves financial data for a user's portfolio.
- The /login endpoint is used to authenticate users with JWT tokens.

Set Up React Frontend: React will be responsible for displaying real-time data on the dashboard. The frontend will fetch financial data from the Flask API and use libraries like **Chart.js** or **Recharts** to visualize the data.
Install React Dependencies:
bash
CopyEdit

```bash
npx create-react-app financial-dashboard

cd financial-dashboard

npm install axios recharts
```

Creating a React Component to Fetch Financial Data: Create a React component that fetches portfolio data and displays it using **Recharts**.
Example React Component (Portfolio.js):
javascript
CopyEdit

```javascript
import React, { useState, useEffect } from 'react';
```

```javascript
import axios from 'axios';

import { LineChart, Line, XAxis, YAxis, CartesianGrid, Tooltip, Legend,
ResponsiveContainer } from 'recharts';


function Portfolio() {

  const [portfolioData, setPortfolioData] = useState([]);

  const [authToken, setAuthToken] = useState(localStorage.getItem('token'));


  useEffect(() => {

   if (authToken) {

     axios.get('http://localhost:5000/portfolio', {

       headers: {

         Authorization: `Bearer ${authToken}`

       }

     })

     .then(response => {

       setPortfolioData(response.data);

     })

     .catch(error => {

       console.error("There was an error fetching portfolio data!", error);

     });

   }
```

```
}, [authToken]);

return (
  <div>
    <h1>Portfolio Overview</h1>
    <ResponsiveContainer width="100%" height={300}>
      <LineChart data={portfolioData}>
        <XAxis dataKey="stock_name" />
        <YAxis />
        <CartesianGrid strokeDasharray="3 3" />
        <Tooltip />
        <Legend />
        <Line type="monotone" dataKey="quantity" stroke="#8884d8" />
      </LineChart>
    </ResponsiveContainer>
  </div>
);
}

export default Portfolio;
```

- o This component fetches the portfolio data from the Flask API and uses **Recharts** to display the stock quantities in a line chart.

Authentication with JWT: In the React app, store the JWT token in **localStorage** after the user logs in, and send this token in the Authorization header for authenticated requests.

Test the Full-Stack Application: Use **Postman** to test the Flask API, ensuring that the authentication and data retrieval endpoints work as expected. Then, run the React app using:
bash
CopyEdit
npm start

Building a **financial dashboard** with Flask and React enables you to create dynamic, data-driven applications that allow users to track their portfolios and visualize financial data. Flask provides the backend logic and data management, while React handles real-time data fetching and dynamic chart rendering, creating an interactive and scalable application. With features like JWT authentication, API data fetching, and charting libraries, this setup can be extended to include real-time market updates, user authentication, and more advanced analytics.

Chapter 16: Flask for Microservices and Serverless

16.1 Introduction to Microservices Architecture

Microservices architecture is an approach to software development where a system is broken down into a collection of loosely coupled, independently deployable services. Each microservice typically corresponds to a specific business function and is designed to perform a distinct task. These services can communicate with each other through well-defined APIs, most often using HTTP-based RESTful APIs or messaging queues.

Key Characteristics of Microservices:

1. **Modularity**: Microservices are self-contained, and each one has its own specific domain and functionality. This makes it easier to maintain, update, and scale individual services.
2. **Independence**: Each service is independently deployable, which enables continuous deployment and scaling. This autonomy allows teams to develop and deploy services independently.
3. **Technology Agnostic**: Since microservices communicate over standard APIs, different services within the same architecture can be written in different programming languages or use different databases and tools.
4. **Scalability**: Microservices allow for granular scaling. You can scale specific services independently based on demand, which improves resource utilization and efficiency.
5. **Resilience**: A failure in one service doesn't necessarily mean a failure for the whole system. The system can continue operating, and the faulty service can be isolated, restarted, or replaced.

Benefits of Microservices Architecture:

- **Faster Development and Deployment**: Teams can work on different services simultaneously, reducing time to market.
- **Easier to Scale**: Individual services can be scaled based on demand rather than scaling the entire application.
- **Improved Fault Isolation**: Faults in one microservice don't propagate to others, making the system more resilient.

- **Flexible Technology Stack**: Each service can use the most suitable technology, language, or framework for its specific task.

Challenges with Microservices:

- **Complexity in Management**: As the number of microservices grows, it can become difficult to manage communication, versioning, and deployment.
- **Increased Latency**: Inter-service communication may involve network calls, potentially introducing latency.
- **Data Consistency**: Maintaining consistency across services and databases can be more complex in a microservices environment.

Microservices Communication:

In microservices architecture, services communicate with each other through RESTful APIs, GraphQL, or messaging queues like **RabbitMQ**, **Kafka**, or **AWS SQS**. RESTful communication is often preferred due to its simplicity and wide usage.

Use Cases for Microservices:

- **E-commerce platforms**: Microservices are ideal for e-commerce applications, where services like product catalog, inventory, payment processing, and order management can be split into independent services.
- **Financial services**: In banking or payment systems, microservices can handle user authentication, transaction processing, fraud detection, and compliance.
- **Media and content platforms**: Content delivery, user authentication, and media encoding services can be decoupled for better scalability and performance.

16.2 Using Flask for Microservices

Flask, as a lightweight micro-framework, is an excellent choice for building microservices. Its minimalism and flexibility make it an ideal candidate for creating RESTful APIs, which are central to microservice communication. In this section, we will explore how to use Flask to build microservices and how to handle the core challenges involved.

Setting Up a Simple Flask Microservice

When building a microservice with Flask, the primary goal is to expose simple, well-defined HTTP APIs for each service to interact with other services in the system. These APIs handle requests from clients or other services and return JSON responses.

Creating a Simple Flask Microservice: Here is a basic example of a Flask microservice that provides a product catalog API for an e-commerce platform.
Install Flask:
bash
CopyEdit
```
pip install Flask
```
Flask Microservice Code:
python
CopyEdit
```
from flask import Flask, jsonify

app = Flask(__name__)

products = [
    {'id': 1, 'name': 'Product A', 'price': 100},
    {'id': 2, 'name': 'Product B', 'price': 150},
    {'id': 3, 'name': 'Product C', 'price': 200}
]

@app.route('/api/products', methods=['GET'])
def get_products():
    return jsonify(products)

if __name__ == '__main__':
    app.run(debug=True, host='0.0.0.0', port=5000)
```

In this example:
- o The /api/products endpoint returns a list of products in JSON format.
- o The service exposes a simple API that can be consumed by other microservices or clients.

Running the Flask Microservice: To run the Flask app, simply execute the following command:
bash

```
python app.py
```

The service will be available at http://localhost:5000/api/products, and clients can retrieve the product catalog by sending a GET request to this endpoint.

Microservice Architecture with Flask

API Gateway: In a microservices environment, an **API Gateway** is typically used to act as a single entry point for all client requests. The gateway handles routing, load balancing, and security, directing requests to the appropriate backend service.
Flask can be used to build a lightweight API Gateway that routes requests to various microservices based on the requested endpoint.

Example API Gateway:
python
```
from flask import Flask, redirect, url_for

app = Flask(__name__)

@app.route('/products')
def products():
    return redirect('http://product-service:5000/api/products')

if __name__ == '__main__':
    app.run(debug=True, host='0.0.0.0', port=8080)
```

In this case, the API Gateway receives requests on /products and redirects them to the product-service running on port 5000.

Service Discovery: In a microservices system, services must discover each other dynamically. Using a service registry (e.g., **Consul** or **Eureka**), each service registers its endpoint, and other services can discover and communicate with it.

Communication between Microservices: Microservices typically communicate using HTTP-based RESTful APIs. Flask can easily create RESTful APIs that interact with other services.
Here's how you can make a **GET** request from one Flask microservice to another:
python
```
import requests
```

285

```
@app.route('/external-api')
def get_external_data():
    response = requests.get('http://other-microservice/api/data')
    return jsonify(response.json())
```

Handling Dependencies and Database Connections

- **Database per Service**: Each microservice can have its own database, ensuring that each service is independent and doesn't share state with others. Flask works well with both **SQL** and **NoSQL** databases, and SQLAlchemy or **Flask-MongoEngine** can be used to interact with these databases.
- **Database Transactions**: Since microservices are decoupled, transactions spanning multiple services (often called **distributed transactions**) can be tricky. Tools like **SAGA** or **Eventual Consistency** can help manage such scenarios.

Scaling Flask Microservices

Flask microservices can be scaled independently depending on the load. For example, if the product catalog service receives a high volume of requests, you can scale it horizontally by adding more instances of the service.

Use container orchestration tools like **Docker** and **Kubernetes** to manage the deployment, scaling, and health of each microservice.

16.3 Flask and Serverless: Deploying to AWS Lambda

Serverless computing allows you to run backend code without managing servers. In this model, you upload your functions to a serverless platform like **AWS Lambda**, and the platform handles scaling, execution, and resource management. Flask, combined with AWS Lambda, can be a powerful tool for building cost-effective, scalable applications that don't require the overhead of traditional server management.

What is AWS Lambda?

AWS Lambda is a serverless compute service provided by **Amazon Web Services (AWS)** that runs your code in response to events. Lambda automatically manages the compute fleet providing a balance of memory, CPU, and storage.

With Lambda, you only pay for the compute time you use—there's no charge when your code isn't running, making it an ideal solution for building event-driven applications like REST APIs.

Flask on AWS Lambda

To deploy a Flask application on AWS Lambda, you need a wrapper that makes Flask compatible with the Lambda execution model. One of the most popular tools to facilitate this is **Zappa** or **AWS Serverless Application Model (SAM)**.

Steps to Deploy Flask with AWS Lambda Using Zappa

Install Zappa: Zappa is a powerful tool that deploys Python applications to AWS Lambda and API Gateway.
bash
CopyEdit

```
pip install zappa
```

Set Up Your Flask Application: Ensure that your Flask application is ready for deployment. Here's a simple example of a Flask app:
python
CopyEdit

```
from flask import Flask, jsonify

app = Flask(__name__)

@app.route('/')
def hello():
    return jsonify(message="Hello from Flask on AWS Lambda!")

if __name__ == '__main__':
    app.run(debug=True)
```

Create Zappa Configuration: Initialize your Zappa project by running:
bash

287

CopyEdit

```
zappa init
```

Zappa will create a zappa_settings.json file where you define deployment settings like AWS region, API Gateway configuration, etc.

Deploy Flask to AWS Lambda: With the configuration in place, deploy your Flask app to AWS Lambda:

bash
CopyEdit

```
zappa deploy production
```

1. Zappa will package your Flask app, upload it to AWS Lambda, and set up API Gateway to route HTTP requests to your Lambda function.
2. **Accessing the API**: After deployment, Zappa will provide you with a public URL. This is the endpoint where your Flask app is now running on AWS Lambda.
3. **Scaling and Event-Driven Architecture**: AWS Lambda automatically scales based on incoming requests, and you only pay for the compute time consumed by the Lambda function. It integrates seamlessly with other AWS services like **S3**, **DynamoDB**, and **SNS** to create a fully serverless, event-driven architecture.

Advantages of Using Flask with AWS Lambda:

- **Cost-Effective**: With serverless architecture, you only pay for the compute resources you use, reducing costs for applications with fluctuating traffic.
- **No Server Management**: AWS Lambda abstracts away the need for provisioning and managing infrastructure, allowing you to focus solely on your code.
- **Automatic Scaling**: Lambda functions automatically scale in response to incoming traffic, without manual intervention.
- **Quick Deployment**: Zappa and similar tools simplify the deployment process, making it easy to get a Flask app running in a serverless environment.

Deploying Flask applications to AWS Lambda allows you to take advantage of the benefits of serverless architecture, including automatic scaling, reduced infrastructure overhead, and cost efficiency. By using tools like **Zappa**, you can quickly deploy your Flask apps to AWS Lambda, making it an excellent choice for APIs, event-driven applications, and microservices that require fast scaling and minimal maintenance. Serverless computing with AWS Lambda and Flask is a powerful combination for building modern, scalable web applications.

16.4 Building Flask APIs for Distributed Systems

Distributed systems consist of multiple independent services that work together to achieve a common goal. These services can run on separate machines or containers, and they communicate with each other over the network. When building APIs for distributed systems with Flask, it's essential to design the system to be resilient, scalable, and capable of handling communication between the services efficiently.

Flask, due to its lightweight nature and flexibility, is a great choice for building APIs in distributed systems, especially when combined with tools like **Message Queues**, **API Gateways**, and **Service Meshes**.

Key Considerations for Building Flask APIs in Distributed Systems

API Gateway: In a distributed system, an **API Gateway** acts as a central entry point for clients to access different services. It routes requests to appropriate microservices, handles load balancing, and can enforce authentication, rate-limiting, or logging. Flask can be used to build an API Gateway that aggregates responses from multiple microservices and forwards them to the client.

Example API Gateway with Flask:
python
CopyEdit

```
from flask import Flask, jsonify, request

import requests


app = Flask(__name__)


@app.route('/api/product/<int:product_id>', methods=['GET'])

def get_product(product_id):
```
289

```python
    product_service_url = f'http://product-service/api/products/{product_id}'
    product_response = requests.get(product_service_url)
    return jsonify(product_response.json())
@app.route('/api/order/<int:order_id>', methods=['GET'])
def get_order(order_id):
    order_service_url = f'http://order-service/api/orders/{order_id}'
    order_response = requests.get(order_service_url)
    return jsonify(order_response.json())


if __name__ == '__main__':
    app.run(debug=True, host='0.0.0.0', port=8080)
```

In this example:
- ○ The Flask API Gateway routes the request to different microservices (product-service and order-service) based on the URL path.
- ○ The requests library is used to send HTTP requests to other microservices and aggregate their responses.

Service Discovery: In a distributed system, services must dynamically discover each other to communicate. A **Service Registry** (such as **Consul**, **Eureka**, or **Zookeeper**) is often used to register the services when they start and to keep track of their locations. Flask can query this registry to find services dynamically.

Service Discovery Example: Instead of hardcoding the service URL in the Flask application, it can query a **Service Registry** to discover the service endpoint.

python
CopyEdit

```python
import requests


# Query Service Registry (e.g., Consul) for product service
```

```python
service_registry_url = 'http://consul-service:8500/v1/catalog/service/product-service'

response = requests.get(service_registry_url)

product_service_address = response.json()[0]['ServiceAddress']
```

Message Queues: Distributed systems often need to communicate asynchronously, especially when processing tasks that can be done in the background. **Message Queues** (like **RabbitMQ**, **Kafka**, or **Amazon SQS**) are used to decouple services and allow asynchronous communication between them.

Flask can be integrated with these message queues to send and receive messages.

Flask with RabbitMQ Example:

python
CopyEdit
```python
import pika

from flask import Flask, jsonify, request


app = Flask(__name__)


def send_message_to_queue(message):

    connection = pika.BlockingConnection(pika.ConnectionParameters('localhost'))

    channel = connection.channel()

    channel.queue_declare(queue='task_queue', durable=True)

    channel.basic_publish(exchange='',

                routing_key='task_queue',

                body=message,

                properties=pika.BasicProperties(

                    delivery_mode=2,  # Make message persistent
```

```
                    ))

  connection.close()


@app.route('/api/task', methods=['POST'])

def create_task():

  task_data = request.json['task']

  send_message_to_queue(task_data)

  return jsonify({'message': 'Task sent to queue'}), 202


if __name__ == '__main__':

  app.run(debug=True)
```

In this example:
- A Flask endpoint /api/task accepts a task and sends it to a **RabbitMQ** queue.
- Another service can listen to this queue and process the tasks asynchronously.

Challenges in Distributed Systems:

- **Data Consistency**: Ensuring consistency across distributed services is often challenging, and solutions like **Eventual Consistency**, **SAGA**, or **two-phase commit** can help.
- **Latency**: Inter-service communication over the network can introduce latency, so it's important to optimize calls and handle retries gracefully.
- **Fault Tolerance**: Distributed systems must be designed to handle partial failures, and services must be able to recover gracefully. **Circuit Breaker** patterns or retry mechanisms can help in this regard.

16.5 Best Practices for Serverless Flask Applications

Serverless computing abstracts away the infrastructure management and allows developers to focus on writing code that responds to events without worrying about provisioning servers. **AWS Lambda** is a popular platform for running serverless applications, and Flask, when paired with tools like **Zappa**, makes it easy to deploy Python web applications in a serverless environment.

Here are some best practices for developing **Flask applications** in serverless environments:

1. Keep Functions Small and Focused

Serverless functions, such as AWS Lambda functions, are optimized for handling single-purpose tasks. Avoid writing large, monolithic functions. Instead, design your Flask application as a set of small, focused functions that each handle a specific task, such as processing an image or querying a database.

- **Example**: Instead of handling both authentication and data retrieval in a single Lambda function, break them into two functions:
    - One function handles user authentication.
    - Another function retrieves data from the database.

2. Optimize Cold Starts

Cold starts are a known issue in serverless computing. When a function is called for the first time or after a long idle period, the platform needs to initialize the runtime environment, leading to latency. To minimize this, consider the following:

- **Keep functions lightweight**: Avoid large dependencies and unnecessary code.
- **Warm-up Lambda functions**: Use AWS CloudWatch or a third-party service to periodically trigger the Lambda function and keep it "warm" to reduce latency.
- **Use layers**: AWS Lambda supports layers, allowing you to manage shared libraries and avoid bundling them in every function deployment.

3. Use Event-Driven Architecture

Serverless functions are triggered by events, such as HTTP requests (via API Gateway), changes to files (via S3), or updates to a database (via DynamoDB Streams). Design your Flask application around these events:

- **API Gateway** can trigger functions based on HTTP requests.
- **S3 events** can trigger functions when files are uploaded.
- **DynamoDB Streams** can trigger functions when there are changes to a database.

Using event-driven architecture, you can easily decouple components of your system, ensuring scalability and flexibility.

4. Manage State with External Services

Serverless functions are stateless, meaning they do not retain information between invocations. To manage state:

- **Use databases** (like **DynamoDB** or **RDS**) to store user sessions or application state.
- **Leverage Amazon S3** to store large files or media.
- **Use Redis or DynamoDB for caching** to minimize database load and improve performance.

5. Monitor and Log Lambda Functions

While running in a serverless environment, it is crucial to monitor the performance of your Flask API. AWS provides **CloudWatch Logs** and **CloudWatch Metrics** for tracking Lambda invocations and performance metrics. Set up custom logging to capture errors, performance metrics, and the health of your functions.

- Use **Flask's built-in logging** to capture logs and send them to AWS CloudWatch.
- Set up **CloudWatch Alarms** to notify you if something goes wrong, such as high error rates or cold start latency.

6. Secure Your Serverless Application

Security in a serverless environment is just as important as any traditional infrastructure. Consider these security best practices:

- **Use AWS IAM Roles**: Assign minimum necessary permissions to your Lambda functions to follow the principle of least privilege.
- **Use API Gateway for Authentication**: Implement API Gateway with **AWS Cognito** for user authentication or integrate third-party services like **OAuth** to secure your APIs.

- **Enable Encryption**: Use **AWS KMS** to encrypt sensitive data stored in **S3**, **DynamoDB**, or **RDS**.

7. Optimize Costs

One of the advantages of serverless is cost efficiency; you only pay for the compute time you use. However, it's still important to optimize for costs:

- **Keep function execution time short**: Minimize the runtime of each function to reduce costs.
- **Use appropriate memory allocation**: Allocate just enough memory for your function to run efficiently. Over-allocating memory can unnecessarily increase costs.
- **Monitor usage**: Use AWS cost management tools to monitor and optimize the cost of your serverless functions.

16.6 Securing Microservices with Flask

Securing microservices is critical, as each microservice potentially exposes sensitive data and functionality. Flask, combined with best practices for authentication, encryption, and service-to-service communication, can ensure that your microservices remain secure and resilient to attacks.

Key Security Practices for Microservices:

1. **Authentication and Authorization**:
   - **JWT Authentication**: Use **JWT (JSON Web Tokens)** for service-to-service authentication. JWT is ideal for stateless authentication in microservices because it allows services to verify the identity of a user without needing to store sessions.
   - **OAuth**: For third-party service integrations, use OAuth to manage secure access and permissions.
   - **API Gateway Authentication**: Use an API Gateway to centralize authentication and authorization, allowing only authenticated requests to reach the microservices.

2. **TLS/SSL Encryption**:
   - **Encrypt Communication**: Ensure that all communication between microservices and between the client and the API Gateway is encrypted using **TLS (Transport Layer Security)**.
   - **Use HTTPS**: Always use HTTPS for sensitive data transmission, ensuring that data is protected in transit.
3. **Role-Based Access Control (RBAC)**:
   - **Limit Service Access**: Use **Role-Based Access Control (RBAC)** to restrict access to microservices based on roles. This ensures that only authorized users and services can interact with certain parts of the system.
   - **Flask-Principal**: Integrate **Flask-Principal** for managing user roles and permissions.
4. **API Rate Limiting**:
   - **Prevent DDoS Attacks**: Implement API rate limiting to prevent abuse and denial-of-service (DoS) attacks. Tools like **Flask-Limiter** can be used to set rate limits for each API endpoint.
   - **API Gateway Rate Limiting**: Use the API Gateway to enforce rate limits for all incoming requests, preventing overload on microservices.
5. **Service-to-Service Communication Security**:
   - **Mutual TLS (mTLS)**: Use **mTLS** to authenticate and encrypt communication between services within a microservice architecture. mTLS ensures that both the client and server are authenticated using certificates.
   - **Secure Service Discovery**: Use secure service discovery mechanisms, such as **Consul** or **Eureka**, to ensure that only trusted services can communicate with each other.
6. **Logging and Monitoring**:
   - **Centralized Logging**: Implement centralized logging to track security-related events such as failed login attempts, unauthorized access attempts, and service errors.
   - **Prometheus and Grafana**: Use **Prometheus** and **Grafana** to monitor microservices performance and alert on suspicious activities or security threats.
7. **Penetration Testing and Vulnerability Scanning**:
   - **Regular Security Audits**: Perform regular penetration testing on your Flask microservices to identify potential security weaknesses.

- **Automated Vulnerability Scanning**: Use tools like **OWASP ZAP** or **Snyk** to scan your application dependencies for known vulnerabilities.

Securing Flask microservices requires implementing a comprehensive approach to authentication, authorization, communication encryption, and access control. By combining Flask's flexibility with best security practices such as JWT, mTLS, RBAC, and rate limiting, you can protect your microservices from unauthorized access, ensure data confidentiality, and maintain the integrity of the system

Chapter 17: Bonus Resources and Tools

17.1 Code Repositories and Project Templates

When developing applications with Flask, leveraging existing code repositories and project templates can significantly expedite development, increase productivity, and ensure best practices are followed. These resources can provide you with well-structured Flask applications, reusable components, and pre-configured settings that allow you to focus on building features rather than reinventing the wheel.

1. GitHub and GitLab Repositories

GitHub and **GitLab** are the most popular platforms for storing and sharing code repositories. Both platforms offer public and private repositories, allowing developers to share their code, collaborate, and contribute to open-source projects.

Here are some highly recommended repositories and templates to get started with Flask:

- **Flask Mega-Tutorial**: A comprehensive, step-by-step guide to building a complete application using Flask. It's an ideal starting point for beginners and covers various aspects of Flask, including user authentication, databases, and deployment.
  - GitHub Repository: https://github.com/miguelgrinberg/microblog
- **Flask Restful API Template**: A Flask-based template designed for building RESTful APIs. This template provides a basic structure for creating APIs, handling authentication, logging, and error handling.
  - GitHub Repository: https://github.com/Flask-RESTful-Template/flask-restful-api-template
- **Cookiecutter Flask**: A project template that helps you get started with Flask quickly by providing a cookiecutter template. It includes pre-configured settings for things like project structure, testing, and deployment.
  - GitHub Repository: https://github.com/cookiecutter/cookiecutter-flask
- **Flask Boilerplate**: A ready-to-use Flask application template designed to quickly set up a web application. It comes with user authentication, database integration, and various configuration files.
  - GitHub Repository: https://github.com/cosmic-byte/flask-boilerplate

By using these repositories, developers can accelerate their learning and application development by having a solid foundation to build on.

2. Project Templates

In addition to code repositories, project templates are a great way to start working on Flask applications quickly. These templates are fully-configured projects that adhere to best practices, allowing you to get started without worrying about basic setup.

Popular Flask Project Templates:

- **Flask App Starter**: A project template that includes the basic structure of a Flask application, including file handling, form validation, and error handling. It's perfect for building both small and large-scale Flask applications.
  - GitHub Template: https://github.com/realpython/flask-app-starter
- **Flask-SQLAlchemy Template**: A template that includes integration with Flask-SQLAlchemy, designed for building database-backed applications. It also features common patterns for handling database queries and migrations.
  - GitHub Template:
    https://github.com/jakevdp/Flask-SQLAlchemy-template

Using project templates not only saves time but also ensures that you are following best practices in terms of project structure, database handling, and deployment.

17.2 Accessing a Community for Flask Developers

Flask is widely adopted by developers across the globe, and engaging with the community is a great way to expand your knowledge, solve problems, and stay up to date with the latest trends and practices in Flask development. There are numerous forums, Slack groups, and communities where developers can interact, ask questions, share resources, and contribute to the Flask ecosystem.

1. Stack Overflow

Stack Overflow is one of the largest developer communities on the web. With a large number of Flask-related questions, Stack Overflow is an excellent resource for getting answers to your Flask development problems. You can ask questions, search for existing solutions, and learn from experienced developers.

- Stack Overflow Flask Tag: https://stackoverflow.com/questions/tagged/flask

2. Flask Discord and Slack Communities

Flask has several active communities on **Discord** and **Slack** where developers engage in discussions, share ideas, and help each other troubleshoot issues.

- **Flask Discord**: Join the official Flask Discord community to talk with other Flask developers in real-time, ask questions, and share your knowledge.
  - Invitation Link: Flask Discord
- **Flask Slack**: Slack is another platform where Flask developers can engage in discussions, share resources, and contribute to open-source Flask projects.
  - Invitation Link: Flask Slack Community

3. Flask Google Groups

Google Groups is a place where developers can join mailing lists and participate in discussions on various topics related to Flask. This platform allows for in-depth discussions about Flask-related topics and serves as a place to ask questions, share resources, and get answers from the community.

- Flask Google Group: https://groups.google.com/forum/#!forum/flask

4. Reddit - Flask Subreddit

The **Flask subreddit** is an excellent place for Flask developers to discuss best practices, share resources, and ask questions about using Flask in production environments.

- Flask Subreddit: https://www.reddit.com/r/flask/

5. Flask Documentation and Flask Users Group

- **Flask Documentation**: The official Flask documentation is a great starting point for new developers. It provides in-depth tutorials, installation guides, and best practices.
  - Official Flask Docs: https://flask.palletsprojects.com/
- **Flask Users Group**: The Flask Users Group is an online forum for Flask developers to share solutions, discuss Flask updates, and ask questions.
  - Flask Users Group: https://www.mail-archive.com/flask@python.org/

17.3 Useful Flask API Tools and Extensions

Flask's simplicity is one of its core strengths, but as your Flask application grows, you'll need additional tools and extensions to handle more complex tasks such as authentication, database management, and API creation. Thankfully, Flask has a rich ecosystem of extensions that provide robust solutions for many common challenges. Below are some of the most useful Flask extensions for building powerful APIs.

1. Flask-SQLAlchemy

Flask-SQLAlchemy is an extension for Flask that adds support for **SQLAlchemy**, the most popular ORM (Object-Relational Mapping) tool for Python. It allows Flask applications to interact with relational databases like MySQL, PostgreSQL, and SQLite.

- **Key Features**:
  - ○ ORM-based database management
  - ○ Simplifies database schema creation and querying
  - ○ Provides a simple way to integrate migrations using **Flask-Migrate**

Installation:
bash
CopyEdit
```
pip install flask-sqlalchemy
```

2. Flask-RESTful

Flask-RESTful is an extension for building REST APIs quickly and with minimal effort. It adds simple abstractions for creating resources and handling HTTP methods like GET, POST, PUT, DELETE, etc.

- **Key Features**:
  - ○ Defines resources in an intuitive way
  - ○ Handles request parsing and input validation
  - ○ Supports output formatting (JSON, XML, etc.)

Installation:
bash
CopyEdit
```
pip install flask-restful
```

Example Usage:
python
CopyEdit
```
from flask_restful import Api, Resource

api = Api(app)

class HelloWorld(Resource):
    def get(self):
        return {'message': 'Hello, World!'}

api.add_resource(HelloWorld, '/')
```

3. Flask-JWT-Extended

Flask-JWT-Extended is an extension for Flask that simplifies the process of using **JSON Web Tokens (JWT)** for authentication and authorization in your API. It helps secure routes and manage tokens.

- **Key Features**:
  - Easy handling of JWT for authentication
  - Allows token creation, verification, and management
  - Supports token expiration and refresh functionality

Installation:
bash
CopyEdit
```
pip install flask-jwt-extended
```

4. Flask-CORS

Flask-CORS is an extension that allows cross-origin resource sharing (CORS) in Flask applications. It is especially useful when you want to allow frontend applications running on a different domain to interact with your API.

- **Key Features**:
  - Easy to set up for handling cross-origin requests
  - Configurable for specific routes or globally

Installation:
bash
CopyEdit
pip install flask-cors

5. Flask-Marshmallow

Flask-Marshmallow integrates **Marshmallow**, a popular object serialization and validation library, with Flask. It simplifies serializing complex data types (like ORM models) to JSON and deserializing JSON back to Python objects.

- **Key Features**:
    - Provides easy-to-use serialization for Python objects
    - Can be used for request validation and response formatting
    - Works well with Flask-SQLAlchemy models

Installation:
bash
CopyEdit
pip install flask-marshmallow

6. Flask-Migrate

Flask-Migrate is an extension for handling database migrations in Flask applications. It works with **Alembic**, a database migration tool, to help you manage changes to your database schema.

- **Key Features**:
    - Easily manage database schema changes
    - Supports version control for your database
    - Works well with Flask-SQLAlchemy

Installation:
bash
CopyEdit
pip install flask-migrate

7. Flask-SocketIO

Flask-SocketIO is an extension that allows Flask to handle **WebSockets** and implement real-time bidirectional communication between clients and the server.

- **Key Features**:
    - Easily integrate WebSockets into Flask apps
    - Support for events and broadcasting messages
    - Works well for real-time applications like chat systems or live updates

Installation:
bash
CopyEdit
pip install flask-socketio

Flask's ecosystem of tools and extensions is extensive and provides solutions for many common tasks in web development, especially for API development. Extensions like **Flask-SQLAlchemy**, **Flask-RESTful**, **Flask-JWT-Extended**, and others make it easy to handle everything from database management to authentication and real-time communication. By leveraging these tools, developers can build robust, scalable, and secure Flask applications with minimal effort.

17.4 Bonus Chapter: Using Flask with Machine Learning APIs

Integrating Flask with **Machine Learning (ML) APIs** allows you to build intelligent applications that can process and predict data using trained models. Flask can act as the interface for deploying machine learning models as REST APIs, making it easier to integrate them into web or mobile applications. This section will show how to use Flask to create APIs that serve machine learning models, allowing you to perform tasks such as prediction, classification, and data analysis.

1. Why Use Flask for Machine Learning APIs?

Flask is an excellent choice for deploying machine learning models for several reasons:

- **Simplicity**: Flask provides a lightweight and flexible framework for setting up a web API to interact with machine learning models. It's easy to integrate with Python-based machine learning libraries such as **scikit-learn**, **TensorFlow**, or **PyTorch**.
- **Rapid Prototyping**: Flask allows you to quickly create RESTful APIs to serve ML models, making it a great tool for testing and iterating on your models in real-world applications.
- **Scalability**: Flask, combined with containerization tools like Docker, can be scaled easily to serve multiple model instances or run as part of a larger microservices architecture.

2. Serving Machine Learning Models with Flask

To create an ML API with Flask, the general process involves:

1. **Training a Model**: Train a machine learning model using a library like **scikit-learn**, **TensorFlow**, or **PyTorch**.
2. **Pickling the Model**: Serialize the trained model using Python's pickle or joblib module to save it for later use.
3. **Building the Flask API**: Set up an API endpoint in Flask to accept input, run predictions, and return the results.
4. **Serving the Model**: Use Flask to serve the trained model and accept HTTP requests (e.g., via POST) with input data for predictions.

3. Example: Creating a Machine Learning API with Flask

Let's walk through an example of deploying a simple machine learning model with Flask. In this example, we'll use **scikit-learn** to train a classification model, save it, and then serve it with Flask.

Step 1: Train a Simple Model with Scikit-learn

python

305

CopyEdit

```python
from sklearn.datasets import load_iris
from sklearn.model_selection import train_test_split
from sklearn.ensemble import RandomForestClassifier
import joblib

# Load the dataset
data = load_iris()
X = data.data
y = data.target

# Split the data into training and testing sets
X_train, X_test, y_train, y_test = train_test_split(X, y, test_size=0.2, random_state=42)

# Train a RandomForestClassifier
model = RandomForestClassifier()
model.fit(X_train, y_train)

# Save the model to a file
joblib.dump(model, 'iris_model.pkl')
```

In this step:

- We load the Iris dataset and train a RandomForestClassifier on it.
- The model is then serialized using **joblib** and saved to a file (iris_model.pkl).

Step 2: Set Up Flask API to Serve the Model

Now, let's create a Flask application that loads the saved model and serves it via an API endpoint.

python

CopyEdit

```python
from flask import Flask, request, jsonify

import joblib

import numpy as np


app = Flask(__name__)


# Load the trained model

model = joblib.load('iris_model.pkl')


@app.route('/predict', methods=['POST'])

def predict():

    # Get the input data from the request

    data = request.get_json()

    features = np.array(data['features']).reshape(1, -1)


    # Make a prediction
```

```
prediction = model.predict(features)


# Return the prediction as JSON

return jsonify({'prediction': int(prediction[0])})


if __name__ == '__main__':

    app.run(debug=True)
```

In this code:

- We load the pre-trained **RandomForestClassifier** using joblib.load().
- The /predict endpoint accepts POST requests with JSON data containing feature values (in this case, the Iris flower features).
- The features are converted into a **NumPy array**, reshaped as necessary, and passed to the model's predict() method.
- The prediction is returned as a JSON response.

Step 3: Testing the API

Run the Flask Application: Start the Flask server by running:
bash
CopyEdit
```
python app.py
```


Make a POST Request to the API: Using **Postman** or **cURL**, you can send a POST request to the /predict endpoint with sample input data:
Example cURL command:
bash
CopyEdit
```
curl -X POST -H "Content-Type: application/json" \
```

```
-d '{"features": [5.1, 3.5, 1.4, 0.2]}' \
```

http://localhost:5000/predict

The response will be:
json
CopyEdit
{"prediction": 0}

This output indicates that the model has predicted the Iris flower to be of class 0 (Setosa).

17.5 Further Reading and Resources

While this book has covered a broad spectrum of topics related to Flask and API development, the Flask ecosystem is vast, and there's always more to learn. Here are some resources to continue your Flask journey and stay up-to-date with new developments.

1. Official Flask Documentation

The official Flask documentation is the best place to start for understanding the core concepts, installation, and usage of Flask. It also includes guides for deploying and scaling Flask applications.

- **Link**: Flask Documentation

2. Flask Mega-Tutorial by Miguel Grinberg

Miguel Grinberg's **Flask Mega-Tutorial** is a fantastic resource that walks you through building real-world applications using Flask. It's a great way to deepen your knowledge and gain hands-on experience with Flask.

- **Link**: Flask Mega-Tutorial

3. Real Python Flask Tutorials

Real Python is a popular website that offers in-depth tutorials on Python and Flask. Their **Flask tutorials** range from beginner to advanced levels and cover a wide variety of topics, from basic API development to more advanced Flask concepts.

- **Link**: Real Python Flask Tutorials

4. Flask Extension Documentation

Flask has a robust ecosystem of extensions that provide functionality for authentication, databases, form handling, and much more. Here are some popular Flask extensions and their documentation:

- **Flask-SQLAlchemy**: Flask-SQLAlchemy Documentation
- **Flask-RESTful**: Flask-RESTful Documentation
- **Flask-JWT-Extended**: Flask-JWT-Extended Documentation
- **Flask-CORS**: Flask-CORS Documentation

5. Flask Deployment Resources

Once you're ready to deploy your Flask applications, it's important to understand the deployment process. The following resources will guide you through deploying Flask to various platforms, including **Heroku**, **AWS**, and **Docker**:

- **Deploying Flask on Heroku**: Heroku Flask Deployment Guide
- **Deploying Flask on AWS Lambda**: Zappa Documentation
- **Flask Deployment with Docker**: Dockerizing Flask Applications

6. Books on Flask and Web Development

If you prefer reading books for more comprehensive coverage on Flask and web development, here are a couple of excellent titles:

- **"Flask Web Development" by Miguel Grinberg**: This book provides a thorough introduction to building web applications with Flask, covering both beginner and intermediate topics.
- **"Mastering Flask Web Development" by Daniel Gaspar**: This book dives deeper into advanced Flask topics and provides guidance on building production-ready applications.

7. Community and Support

Engaging with the Flask community is a great way to learn, share knowledge, and get help. Here are some online communities where you can connect with other Flask developers:

- **Flask Google Group**: Flask Google Group
- **Flask Subreddit**: Flask on Reddit
- **Stack Overflow**: Search for Flask-related questions on Stack Overflow.

8. Flask on Twitter and Blogs

Stay updated with the latest news, releases, and tutorials related to Flask by following the official Flask Twitter account and relevant blogs:

- **Flask Twitter**: @Flask
- **Flask Blog**: Flask Blog

Flask is a powerful and versatile framework that enables you to build scalable web applications and APIs quickly and efficiently. The resources listed above will help you further expand your Flask knowledge and gain hands-on experience as you continue your development journey. Whether you're building small web applications or large-scale distributed systems, Flask provides the tools you need to create high-quality, maintainable applications.

Appendix

A1: Quick Setup Guide for Flask Development

Setting up a Flask development environment is straightforward and can be done in just a few steps. This guide will help you get started quickly with Flask on your local machine.

Step 1: Install Python

Ensure you have Python 3.6 or higher installed on your system. You can download the latest version of Python from the official website:

- Download Python

Step 2: Install Flask

You can install Flask using **pip**, the Python package installer. It's recommended to use a **virtual environment** for Flask projects to avoid conflicts with system-wide packages.

1. **Set up a virtual environment**:
   bash
   CopyEdit
   ```
   python3 -m venv venv
   ```

2. **Activate the virtual environment**:

On macOS/Linux:
bash
CopyEdit
```
source venv/bin/activate
```

   - On Windows:
     bash
     CopyEdit
     ```
     .\venv\Scripts\activate
     ```

3. **Install Flask**:
bash
CopyEdit
pip install Flask

Step 3: Create a Simple Flask Application

Create a file named app.py and write the following code to test your Flask installation:

python
CopyEdit
```python
from flask import Flask

app = Flask(__name__)

@app.route('/')
def hello_world():
    return 'Hello, World!'

if __name__ == '__main__':
    app.run(debug=True)
```

Step 4: Run the Application

In your terminal, navigate to the folder where app.py is located and run the following command:

bash
CopyEdit
```bash
python app.py
```

Your Flask application should now be running at http://localhost:5000. Open this URL in your browser to see the "Hello, World!" message.

Step 5: Install Additional Packages

You can install additional Flask extensions as needed for your project. For example, if you want to use Flask-SQLAlchemy for database management:

bash
CopyEdit
```
pip install flask-sqlalchemy
```

A2: Flask API Security Checklist

Securing your Flask API is essential to protect sensitive data and ensure safe communication between clients and servers. Here's a checklist to help you secure your Flask-based API:

1. Authentication and Authorization

- **Use Strong Authentication**: Implement user authentication using methods like **JWT (JSON Web Tokens)** or **OAuth**.
- **Role-Based Access Control (RBAC)**: Implement RBAC to restrict access based on user roles and permissions.
- **Token Expiration**: Set token expiration and refresh strategies to mitigate the risks of long-lived tokens.

2. Input Validation

- **Validate User Input**: Use libraries like **Marshmallow** or **WTForms** to validate input and avoid invalid or malicious data.
- **Sanitize Input**: Always sanitize inputs to prevent **SQL injection** or **XSS (Cross-Site Scripting)** attacks.

3. Secure Data Transmission

- **Use HTTPS**: Ensure all API endpoints are served over HTTPS to encrypt data in transit.
- **Implement HSTS**: Use **HTTP Strict Transport Security (HSTS)** to enforce the use of HTTPS.

4. Error Handling

- **Avoid Detailed Error Messages**: Do not expose stack traces or detailed error messages to the client. Instead, log errors and return generic messages to the user.
- **Use Custom Error Pages**: Implement custom error pages to handle common errors like 404 (not found) or 500 (server error).

5. Rate Limiting

- **Rate Limiting**: Implement rate limiting using tools like **Flask-Limiter** to prevent DDoS (Distributed Denial of Service) attacks.
- **Block Suspicious IPs**: Monitor and block IP addresses that repeatedly exceed the rate limits.

6. Secure Session Management

- **Use Secure Cookies**: Set **secure, HttpOnly**, and **SameSite** flags for cookies to protect against cross-site scripting (XSS) and cross-site request forgery (CSRF).
- **Session Expiry**: Set short session expiry times to minimize the impact of stolen sessions.

7. CORS (Cross-Origin Resource Sharing)

- **Restrict CORS**: Limit the domains that can access your API by configuring **CORS** headers. Use **Flask-CORS** for better control.

8. Logging and Monitoring

- **Log API Access**: Implement logging to capture all incoming API requests and responses.
- **Monitor for Suspicious Activity**: Set up alerting for unusual access patterns or security incidents.

A3: Performance Optimization Checklist

Optimizing the performance of your Flask API ensures that it can handle a high volume of requests efficiently while providing a smooth user experience. Here's a checklist for performance optimization:

1. Efficient Database Queries

- **Use Database Indexes**: Ensure that indexes are used on frequently queried columns to speed up searches.
- **Use Lazy Loading**: Avoid loading unnecessary data from the database; use **lazy loading** to only load data when it's needed.
- **Database Query Optimization**: Avoid N+1 query problems and use **SQLAlchemy** or **raw SQL** to write efficient queries.

2. Caching

- **Cache API Responses**: Use **Flask-Caching** to cache frequent API responses and reduce the load on your database.
- **Cache Expiration**: Set proper expiration times for cached data to ensure that it stays up-to-date.

3. Use Asynchronous Processing

- **Background Tasks**: Use **Celery** to handle long-running tasks asynchronously and offload them from the main request-response cycle.
- **Queue Management**: Use a task queue to manage background jobs effectively.

4. Optimize Static Files

- **Minimize and Compress Assets**: Minimize and compress JavaScript, CSS, and image files using tools like **Flask-Assets**.
- **Use a CDN**: Serve static files from a Content Delivery Network (CDN) to reduce load times for users across the globe.

5. Use Load Balancing

- **Horizontal Scaling**: Scale your Flask app horizontally by running multiple instances behind a load balancer.

- **Session Stickiness**: If you use sessions, ensure session stickiness to route requests from the same user to the same instance.

6. Profiling and Monitoring

- **Use Profiling Tools**: Profile your application using tools like **Flask-Profiler** or **cProfile** to identify bottlenecks.
- **Monitor with Prometheus**: Use **Prometheus** or **New Relic** to monitor performance and identify slow endpoints.

A4: Common Flask API Errors and Solutions

When working with Flask APIs, you may encounter various errors. Here's a list of common Flask API errors and their solutions:

1. 404 Not Found

- **Cause**: The requested route does not exist.
- **Solution**: Check if the route exists in your Flask app and make sure you are using the correct HTTP method (GET, POST, etc.).

2. 400 Bad Request

- **Cause**: The request was malformed, or required data was missing.
- **Solution**: Validate input data using libraries like **Marshmallow** or **WTForms** to ensure correct input before processing.

3. 401 Unauthorized

- **Cause**: The client failed to authenticate with the server.
- **Solution**: Check the authentication method (e.g., **JWT**, **OAuth**) and ensure the client provides valid credentials or tokens.

4. 500 Internal Server Error

- **Cause**: An unexpected error occurred on the server.
- **Solution**: Check the server logs for more details on the error and implement proper error handling and logging to track down issues.

5. CSRF Protection Errors

- **Cause**: Cross-Site Request Forgery (CSRF) protection blocked a request.
- **Solution**: Use **Flask-WTF** to generate CSRF tokens and ensure that requests coming from external sites include the proper CSRF token.

6. Database Connection Errors

- **Cause**: The database connection could not be established.
- **Solution**: Ensure that the database server is running, check the database credentials, and verify the connection URL in your Flask configuration.

A5: Glossary of Key Terms

- **Flask**: A lightweight, Python-based web framework used for building web applications and APIs.
- **API (Application Programming Interface)**: A set of protocols that allows different software systems to communicate.
- **JWT (JSON Web Token)**: A compact, URL-safe means of representing claims to be transferred between two parties.
- **ORM (Object-Relational Mapping)**: A programming technique that allows developers to interact with relational databases using object-oriented programming.
- **CORS (Cross-Origin Resource Sharing)**: A mechanism that allows web applications running at one origin to request resources from a different origin.
- **CSRF (Cross-Site Request Forgery)**: An attack that tricks the user into making unwanted requests to a web application where the user is authenticated.

A6: Index

- **Error Handling**: Flask error handling strategies and common issues — Chapter 13.
- **Performance Optimization**: Caching, database query optimization, and load balancing — Chapter 8.
- **Security**: Flask API security measures and best practices — Chapter 6 and A2.

This index allows for quick reference to key topics throughout the book and guides you to the relevant chapters where you can deepen your understanding.